A TASTE OF
ITALY

A TASTE OF
ITALY

···· 100 ····

TRADITIONAL, HOMESTYLE RECIPES

DAMIANO CARRARA

STERLING EPICURE
New York

STERLING EPICURE
New York

An Imprint of Sterling Publishing Co., Inc.
1166 Avenue of the Americas
New York, NY 10036

ISBN 978-1-4549-2647-4

Distributed in Canada by Sterling Publishing Co., Inc.
c/o Canadian Manda Group, 664 Annette Street
Toronto, Ontario, Canada M6S 2C8
Distributed in the United Kingdom by GMC
Distribution Services
Castle Place, 166 High Street, Lewes, East Sussex,
England BN7 1XU
Distributed in Australia by NewSouth Books
45 Beach Street, Coogee, NSW 2034, Australia

For information about custom editions, special sales,
and premium and corporate purchases, please contact
Sterling Special Sales at 800-805-5489 or specialsales@
sterlingpublishing.com.

Manufactured in Canada

10 9 8 7 6 5 4 3 2 1

sterlingpublishing.com

Design by Lorie Pagnozzi
Photos by Lido Vannucchi

CONTENTS

INTRODUCTION

My earliest memories, as a child, are of my father. I remember the aroma of his tomato sauce as it simmered on the stove, and spending mornings standing in his shadow to keep cool as he tended to the vegetables in our garden. Occasionally, my father would pick a ripe tomato or carrot, turn around, and offer it to me. I would scrunch up my nose and yell *no grazie*! At the time, I didn't like to eat my vegetables, like most small children. But years later, as I cook in my own kitchen, and take a bite out of a tomato from my own garden, the memories of those days bring a smile to my face. My family and memories of growing up in my hometown of Lucca, Italy inspired all the recipes in this book. Those memories, moments, laughter, and love are the main ingredients of my life—memories like waking up to the aroma of boiling milk and fresh warm cookies, which my mom, Laura, made for breakfast.

Many times, while I'm cooking, I'm filled with ideas, and remember making fresh pasta like tagliatelle and lasagna with my grandma in our house in the mountains of Bologna.

My grandma Rosita makes amazing simple Italian dishes to feed the family, including a delicious cake that I like to call *Torta Rosita*, which makes everyone smile at holiday gatherings.

Other family members have influenced my cooking technique and knowledge. For example, a lot of the fish dishes and all the vegetarian recipes in this book are from my uncle Vincenzo and his wife Luana. I remember spending weekends with my uncle, making coffee and eating fresh fish from the waters of Massaciuccoli, where he owns a little house on the lake.

Life in Tuscany was beautiful. I grew up in the middle of the countryside, outside the city, surrounded by vegetable gardens, fruit trees, and cornfields. We also had a barn for pigs and cows, and a chicken coop, where my brother and I used to gather warm eggs. We grew most of the food we used to make our meals. In the winter, we spent some time in a small village called Pianaccio, in a mountainous province of Bologna.

Today, our home is on a creek with a small waterfall that rushes past the house. We have a beautiful garden with roses and fresh fruit trees. Next to the house, we keep a supply of wood to stoke our pizza oven and use in the kitchen stove and the fireplace in the living room. There's a pantry below the kitchen, and all the bedrooms are upstairs. In front of the house, there's a well of potable water that flows from the mountains, and our next-door neighbor, Romana, has taught me everything she knows about how to make and prepare pasta.

My experience growing up in Italy in the summertime was very different from the winter months. In fact my mom and dad sacrificed going out and buying things for themselves so that they could send my brother and me to live for three months in the summer with my grandma Liliana and her sister Magda in Lido Di Camaiore, on the coast of Lucca, which has a beautiful sandy beach. I remember arriving at the beginning of summer with pale skin and dark hair and leaving super tanned and with blond hair when it was time to go home. One of my greatest memories of that time is eating a lot of fresh fish and dining under a starry sky at night. My grandma and great aunt cooked for us while we were there, and one of the most amazing things they prepared was a vegetable dish, *Sformato di Cavolfiore*, one of Magda's creations, and which I didn't recognize as cauliflower, a vegetable I did not like as a child. For me, she called the dish *Torta di Verdure Croccante*, a rich, creamy vegetable cake with parmigiano, bread crumbs, and fresh milk. It had a wonderfully crispy texture that I couldn't stop eating.

I came to America in 2009 with the dream of helping my family get a better life, and, after a few years of hard work, my brother Massimiliano joined me here, and we opened our first shop, Carrara Pastries, in Moorpark, California. Two years later, we opened another bakery in Agoura Hills.

Buon appetito!

DAMIANO CARRARA
CEO PRESIDENT
CARRARA PASTRIES, INC.
WWW.CARRARAPASTRIES.COM

A TASTE OF

ITALY

PART 1
SALATO (SAVORY)

ANTIPASTI
(APPETIZERS)

AN ANTIPASTO CAN PROVIDE A GREAT START TO A MEAL AND PRE-
PARES THE PALATE FOR THE REST OF THE MEAL. IT IS MEANT TO STIMU-
LATE YOUR TASTE BUDS AND APPETITE WITHOUT FILLING YOU UP, AND
SETS THE STAGE FOR THE NEXT COURSE. AT HOME, ANTIPASTI WERE
THE FIRST COURSE FOR LUNCHES, DINNER PARTIES, SPECIAL OCCA-
SIONS, AND FESTIVE DAYS, WHEN THE WHOLE FAMILY GATHERED AROUND
THE TABLE. THIS CHAPTER OFFERS A VARIETY OF INGREDIENTS
AND FLAVORS TO COMPLEMENT WHATEVER YOU HAVE IN MIND FOR THE
MAIN COURSE.

·········· A NOTE ON TIMING ··········

For all these recipes, I specify "prep time" and "cooking time."
The total time required to make each dish is the combined
prep time and cooking time.

CAPESANTE IN CROSTA CON GALLETTI E PANCETTA   *4*

(Bread-Crusted Scallops with Crispy Pancetta and Chanterelle Mushrooms)

TARTARA DI FILETTO CON FINOCCHIO E RUCOLA   *7*

(Steak Tartare with Fennel and Arugula)

TARTARA DI FILETTO CON OLIVE   *10*

(Olive Tartare)

TARTARA DI FILETTO CON POMODORINI SECCHI   *11*

(Sun-dried Tomato Tartare)

TARTARA DI TONNO CON MANGO E LAMPONI   *13*

(Tuna Tartare with Mango and Raspberry Caviar)

BRUSCHETTA CON PEPERONATA   *15*

(Mixed Bell Pepper Bruschetta)

POLPETTINE DI CARNE E PATATE   *18*

(Beef and Potato Meatballs)

PIZZETTE DI SFOGLIA   *20*

(Mini Puff Pastry Pizza)

FRITTATINE NELLA PANCETTA   *22*

(Pancetta-Wrapped Egg Frittata)

Capesante in Crosta con Galletti e Pancetta (BREAD-CRUSTED SCALLOPS WITH CRISPY PANCETTA AND CHANTERELLE MUSHROOMS)

WHEN I WAS A KID, MY FAMILY BROUGHT ME TO AN AMAZING RESTAURANT ON THE BEACH IN VIAREGGIO EVERY SUMMER. THIS SCALLOP DISH WAS OUR FAVORITE APPETIZER ON THE MENU. I'VE RE-CREATED IT FROM MEMORY.

PREP TIME: *15 minutes* | COOKING TIME: *20 minutes* | SERVES: *4*

FOR THE BREAD CRUMBS

4 slices leftover bread or any type of stale bread

Salt and pepper to taste

2 sprigs rosemary (without the stems), chopped

8 sage leaves, chopped

Dash of balsamic vinegar

1 tablespoon (15ml) extra virgin olive oil

FOR THE SCALLOPS

12 fresh jumbo scallops

½ pound (230g) chanterelle mushrooms

3–4 tablespoons (45–60ml) extra virgin olive oil, plus extra for drizzling

2 sprigs thyme

2 cloves garlic

Salt and pepper to taste

12 slices pancetta, diced (400g)

¼ cup (60g) butter

INSTRUCTIONS

1. To make the bread crumbs: Start by baking the bread slices at 350°F (180°C) for about 8 minutes. Once the bread is crispy and turns a golden brown, place it in a blender or food processor to reduce it to a fine grind without any visible pieces of bread.

2. In a bowl, add some salt and pepper, the freshly chopped rosemary and sage, a dash of balsamic vinegar, and drizzle a tablespoon (15ml) of olive oil on the bread crumbs, making sure they do not get soggy and clump together. Toss the mixture together, and add more salt and pepper to taste. This bread-crumb mixture needs to be very flavorful.

3. To make the scallops: Clean the scallops by rinsing them under some cold water. Use paper towels to lightly pat them dry. Coat each scallop in the bread-crumb mixture. Be sure to coat them well. Set the scallops aside.

4. Next, rinse the chanterelles under cold water and pat them dry with paper towels. Use a mandoline or a chef's knife to julienne (slice) the mushrooms into thin pieces (this will allow them to cook faster and get nice and crispy).

5. In a nonstick pan on high heat, heat 1–2 tablespoons (15–30ml) of extra virgin olive oil, then add the sprigs of thyme and garlic cloves. Once the mixture is hot, add the mushrooms and salt and pepper to taste, and sauté for at least 5 minutes until the mushrooms start to wilt. Reduce the heat to low and let the mushrooms cook slowly for about 15 minutes, without moving them around, so that they can get crispy.

6. Once the mushrooms are cooked and crispy, remove them from the pan and set them aside on a plate lined with paper towels to absorb any excess oil. Using the same pan, cook the diced pancetta on low heat until it's crispy, about 5 minutes. You want to use the same pan in which the mushrooms were cooked so that the pancetta will absorb the flavor of the mushrooms.

7. To cook the scallops, use a small nonstick pan on medium heat and heat up 2 tablespoons (30ml) of extra virgin olive oil. Make sure the pan is hot before adding the scallops. If the pan is not hot enough, the scallops will stick to the pan and burn. Cook them for about 4 minutes on each side or until they are golden brown.

8. Assembly: Line the mushrooms on a long rectangular plate, and then place a scallop on top of each of the mushrooms. Sprinkle some pancetta on top of each scallop and finish by drizzling a bit of extra virgin olive oil over the entire dish.

Tartara di Filetto con Finocchio e Rucola

(STEAK TARTARE WITH FENNEL AND ARUGULA)

OUR FAMILY USED TO HAVE A GARDEN, AND ONE OF THE VEGETABLES WE GREW—
AND WHICH I LOVED TO EAT—WAS FENNEL. MY PARENTS COOKED IT MANY DIFFERENT
WAYS: THEY ADDED IT TO SALADS, MADE IT INTO A SIDE DISH, OR STUFFED IT INSIDE
MEATS. SOMETIMES WE ATE IT RAW WITH *PINZIMONIO*, A MIXTURE OF EXTRA VIRGIN
OLIVE OIL, BALSAMIC VINEGAR, SALT, AND PEPPER. DELICOUS.

PREP TIME: *15 minutes* | COOKING TIME: *10 minutes* | SERVES: *4*

1 bunch fresh fennel (about 3oz), sliced

4 tablespoons (60ml) olive oil

2 cloves garlic, smashed

3 sprigs fresh thyme, about 1¼ teaspoons (3g)

Salt and pepper to taste

½ pound (230g) filet mignon

2 teaspoons (10ml) Dijon mustard

1 quail egg or fresh farm chicken egg, raw

2 tablespoons (30g) parmigiano, shaved

1 tablespoon (15ml) lemon juice, freshly squeezed, plus juice from 1 lemon wedge

6 ounces (170g) arugula

Crostini (see page 15)

INSTRUCTIONS

1. Clean and rinse the fennel. Remove the stems from the bulb. Use a chef's knife to cut the fennel into thin strands.

2. Heat 3 tablespoons (45ml) of the olive oil in a small pan over medium heat. Add the smashed garlic cloves, fresh thyme, and sliced fennel. Cook the fennel over medium heat for roughly 5 minutes. Add some salt and pepper to taste. While it's cooking, make sure that the fennel caramelizes, without burning, by constantly stirring the fennel, not allowing it to sit still over the heat for too long. When the fennel becomes soft and translucent, and is no longer stringy, remove it from the pan

and lay it flat in strips on a plate. This will help the fennel cool quickly. Once it's cool, chop and mince ¾ of the fennel and set aside the remaining fennel to use as a garnish.

3. Use a sharp chef's knife to remove any tendons or fat from the filet mignon and dice it into small cubes. Chop it well, as you do not want to have any large chunks. Smaller pieces will make the meat tender and easier to chew. Put the meat in a bowl and add ½ tablespoon (7ml) of the oil, mustard, the raw quail egg, shaved parmigiano, 1 tablespoon (15ml) lemon juice, and the previously minced fennel.

4. In a bowl, toss the arugula with 1 tablespoon (15ml) of the olive oil, shaved parmigiano, juice from a lemon wedge, and salt and pepper to taste. Create a bed of arugula on a plate. On top of the arugula, place the tartare in a round cookie cutter, without pressing the meat down too much, to shape the mixture. Remove the cookie cutter and place the remaining unchopped fennel on top of the tartare as a garnish. Add a piece of crostini to the plate and finish the dish by drizzling the rest of the olive oil over the top.

Tartara di Filetto con Olive

(OLIVE TARTARE)

THIS DELICIOUS VARIATION ON THE RECIPE FOR CLASSIC STEAK TARTARE INCLUDES KALAMATA OLIVES.

PREP TIME: *45 minutes* | COOKING TIME: *35 minutes* | SERVES: *4*

12 Kalamata black olives, chopped

½ pound (230g) filet mignon

3–4 tablespoons (45-60ml) extra virgin olive oil

2 teaspoons (14g) Dijon mustard

1 quail egg or fresh farm chicken egg, raw

4 tablespoons (60g) parmigiano, shaved

1 tablespoon (15ml) lemon juice, freshly squeezed, plus juice from 1 lemon wedge

Salt and pepper to taste

6 ounces (170g) arugula

1¼ teaspoons (3g) thyme leaves

2 cloves garlic, smashed

Crostini (see page 15)

INSTRUCTIONS

1. Chop and mince ¾ of the olives and set aside the remaining olives to use as a garnish.

2. Use a sharp chef's knife to remove any tendons or fat from the filet mignon and dice it into small cubes. Chop it well, as you do not want to have any large chunks. Smaller pieces will make the meat tender and easier to chew. Put the meat in a bowl and add ½ tablespoon (7ml) of the oil, mustard, the raw quail egg, 2 tablespoons (30g) shaved parmigiano, 1 tablespoon (15ml) lemon juice, and the previously minced olives.

3. In a bowl, toss the arugula with some of the olive oil, 2 tablespoons (30g) shaved parmigiano, juice from a lemon wedge, and salt and pepper to taste. Create a bed of arugula on a plate. On top of the arugula, place the tartare in a round cookie cutter, without pressing the meat down too much, to shape the mixture. Remove the cookie cutter and place the remaining unchopped olives on top of the tartare as a garnish. Add a piece of crostini to the plate and finish the dish by drizzling the rest of the olive oil over the top.

Tartara di Filetto con Pomodorini Secchi

SUN-DRIED TOMATOES ADD A FRESH TWIST TO THE TRADITIONAL RECIPE FOR STEAK TARTARE.

PREP TIME: *45 minutes* | COOKING TIME: *8 hours, 35 minutes* | SERVES: *4*

INGREDIENTS

8 sun-dried tomatoes

Olive oil, for drizzling

Salt and pepper to taste

Sugar

½ pound (230g) filet mignon

2 tablespoons (30ml) olive oil

2 teaspoons (14g) Dijon mustard

1 quail egg or fresh farm chicken egg, raw

2 tablespoons (30g) parmigiano

1 tablespoon (15ml) lemon juice, freshly squeezed, plus juice from 1 lemon wedge

6 ounces (170g) arugula

Crostini (see page 15)

INSTRUCTIONS

1. To make the sun-dried tomatoes, wash and rinse the tomatoes under cold water and slice each one into 4 pieces. Place them on a baking sheet, and drizzle some olive oil and salt to taste with a pinch of sugar as well. Cook the tomatoes in the oven for about 8 hours at 250°F (120°C). Remove the tomatoes from the oven and let them dry out, uncovered, for a few hours.

2. Chop and mince ¾ of the sun-dried tomatoes and set aside the remaining tomatoes to use as a garnish.

3. Use a sharp chef's knife to remove any tendons or fat from the filet mignon and dice it into small cubes. Chop it well, as you do not want to have any large chunks. Smaller pieces will make the meat tender and easier to chew. Put the meat in a bowl and add ½ tablespoon (7ml) of olive oil, mustard, raw quail egg, shaved parmigiano, lemon juice, and the minced sun-dried tomatoes.

4. In a bowl, toss the arugula with some of the olive oil, shaved parmigiano, juice from a lemon wedge, and salt and pepper to taste. Create a bed of arugula on a plate. On top of the arugula, place the tartare in a round cookie cutter, without pressing the meat down too much, to shape the mixture. Remove the cookie cutter and place the remaining unchopped sun-dried tomatoes on top of the tartare as a garnish. Add a piece of crostini to the plate and finish the dish by drizzling the rest of the olive oil over the top.

Tartare di Tonno con Mango e Lamponi

(TUNA TARTARE WITH MANGO AND RASPBERRY CAVIAR)

MY FAMILY AND I USED TO SPEND EVERY SUMMER AT THE BEACH AND EAT AT A
FANTASTIC RESTAURANT, WHERE THEY SPECIALIZED IN COOKING THE FRESHEST FISH.
OUR FAVORITE WAS TUNA TARTARE. WHEN I WAS A TEENAGER, I ENDED UP GETTING A
JOB AT THAT RESTAURANT, AND ONE OF MY FONDEST MEMORIES WAS GOING TO PICK UP
FRESH TUNA AT THE LOCAL MARKET WITH THE OWNER—IN HIS DUNE BUGGY, OF COURSE!

PREP TIME: *15 minutes* | COOKING TIME: *15 minutes* | SERVES: *4*

FOR THE TUNA TARTARE

½ pound (230g) yellowfin tuna

½ teaspoon (2.5ml) Sriracha sauce

1 teaspoon (5ml) Hoisin sauce

3 tablespoons (45ml) extra virgin olive oil, plus extra for drizzling

1 teaspoon (5ml) soy sauce

1 scallion, chopped

Juice of 1 lime

1 ripe mango, diced

FOR THE RASPBERRY CAVIAR

One 6-ounce (170g) package raspberries

FOR THE TORTILLA CHIPS

One 10-ounce (280g) bag small yellow corn tortillas

Vegetable oil

Salt (equal part)

Cayenne pepper (equal part)

Onion powder (equal part)

Garlic powder (equal part)

Extra virgin olive oil, for drizzling

INSTRUCTIONS

1. To make the tuna: Using a chef's knife, remove any tendons from the tuna. Slice the fish into ¼-inch (6mm) strips. Lay the strips down flat and dice the tuna until it is almost minced. Place the tuna in a bowl and add the Sriracha and Hoisin sauces, the extra virgin olive oil, soy sauce, chopped scallions, and lime juice.

2. Peel and cut a fresh mango into small cubes (make sure to choose a mango whose flesh is golden and ripe so your mango will be sweet). Add the mango to the tuna mixture and set it aside.

3. To make the raspberry caviar: Freeze some raspberries. Once the berries are frozen, tap them gently with a spoon to separate them. Add them to the tuna mixture.

4. To make the tortilla chips: Cut each corn tortilla into 4 triangles. In a shallow pan, deep-fry the tortillas in the vegetable oil at 375°F (190°C) until they are a crisp golden brown. Remove the "chips" from the oil and place them on a plate with paper towels to absorb any excess oil.

5. In another small bowl or container, mix salt, cayenne pepper, onion powder, and garlic powder. Sprinkle the mixture over the chips to season them.

6. To plate the dish, put a spoonful of the tuna tartare mixture on each of the freshly seasoned corn tortilla chips. Finish it off with a drizzle of extra virgin olive oil and enjoy!

Bruschetta con Peperonata

(MIXED BELL PEPPER BRUSCHETTA)

I HAVE BEEN EATING THIS DISH SINCE I WAS A CHILD. WHENEVER WE HAD LEFTOVER BREAD, WE WOULD MAKE BRUSCHETTA AND EAT IT WITH PEPERONATA. THE PERSON WHO INSPIRED THIS RECIPE WAS MY MOM, LAURA—AND THE PEAR IS THE SECRET INGREDIENT THAT NEUTRALIZES THE ACIDITY OF THE PEPPERS AND PREVENTS HEARTBURN.

PREP TIME: *10 minutes* | COOKING TIME: *30 minutes* | SERVES: *4*

FOR THE PEPERONATA

1 yellow bell pepper

1 red bell pepper

1 green bell pepper

1 onion

5 tablespoons (75ml) extra virgin olive oil

Salt and pepper to taste

Pinch crushed red pepper

½ cup (120ml) white wine

One whole ripe Bartlett pear

One 28-ounce (840g) can whole San Marzano tomatoes

FOR THE CROSTINI

1 baguette

Extra virgin olive oil, for drizzling

Salt and pepper to taste

A few arugula leaves for garnish (optional)

INSTRUCTIONS

1. To make the peperonata: Start by washing the bell peppers. Cut the tops off at the stem. Remove the ribs and seeds. Slice the peppers, lengthwise, into about ¼ inch (6mm) thick slices. Set them aside.

2. Slice the onion into long pieces. Heat the olive oil in a nonstick pan over medium heat and toss in the sliced onions. Add some salt and pepper to taste and a pinch of crushed red pepper. Cook the onions until they become golden (about 8 minutes). Add the bell peppers to the onions and mix them together. Cook the bell pepper–and–onion mixture over high heat for 2 minutes, then deglaze the pan by taking it off the stove and adding the wine. Put the pan back on the stove and allow everything to continue to cook.

3. In the meantime, core the pear and slice it into 4 pieces and dice the San Marzano tomatoes. Add the pear and tomatoes to the pan with the bell pepper–and–onion mixture. Cover and simmer the mixture over low to medium heat for 20–25 minutes. Cook the mixture until the peppers are soft, remove the lid, and continue to cook (approximately 5 to 8 minutes) until the tomato sauce has thickened.

4. To make the crostini: Cut a fresh baguette diagonally, into pieces about ½ inch (12mm) thick. Drizzle some olive oil over the baguette slices and sprinkle them with some salt and pepper. Grill each side for about 3 minutes until the bread is crispy and a nice golden brown.

5. Assembly: Place some of the peperonata mixture on top of the crostini. For a nice touch, garnish with some fresh arugula.

Polpettine di Carne e Patate

(BEEF AND POTATO MEATBALLS)

MY FATHER USED TO LOVE MAKING THIS DISH FOR US. YOU CAN EAT THESE
MEATBALLS AS AN APPETIZER OR AN ENTRÉE, OR SERVE THEM WITH A SIDE DISH.
THE POTATOES INSIDE THE MEATBALLS CREATE A SOFT CENTER, AND THE FRESH
HOMEMADE BREAD CRUMBS MAKE THE OUTSIDE WONDERFULLY CRUNCHY.

PREP TIME: *45 minutes* | COOKING TIME: *40 minutes* | SERVES: *4–6*

2 potatoes

1 bunch fresh parsley, minced

¼ cup (20g) parmigiano, grated, plus
    extra for garnish

¼ cup (20g) Pecorino Romano
    cheese, grated

2 eggs

2 cloves garlic, minced

Salt to taste

¾ pound (350g) ground beef

1 cup (125g) bread crumbs

Vegetable oil for frying

A handful (about 3 ounces [85g]) of
    arugula

Extra virgin olive oil, for drizzling

INSTRUCTIONS

1. Boil the potatoes for 20 minutes or until they are soft. When the potatoes are cool,
remove the skins. Mash the potatoes using a potato masher. Mix the minced parsley and
grated cheeses into the potatoes. Set them aside.

2. Add 1 egg, the minced garlic, and a pinch of salt to the ground beef. Do not oversalt
the mixture because pecorino cheese is already salty (if the meat is bland, you can always
add some salt to the meatballs before serving). Mix everything well. Now form the meat
into balls. If the meatballs are big, they will take longer to cook. If they are small, they will
take less time to cook. After you have formed all the meat into balls, dip them in beaten
egg and coat them with bread crumbs.

3. In a small pan, heat the vegetable oil to 350°F (180°C) and fry the meatballs for
about 10 minutes on each side. Remove the meatballs from the oil and transfer them to a
plate lined with paper towels to absorb any excess oil. Serve the meatballs on top of a bed
arugula. Drizzle some olive oil on top and garnish with shaved parmigiano.

Pizzette di Sfoglia

(MINI PUFF PASTRY PIZZAS)

PUFF PASTRY PIZZA IS THE PERFECT RECIPE FOR A PARTY WITH FRIENDS AND LITTLE KIDS. IN ITALY, YOU WILL FIND THAT PIZZETTAS (MINI PIZZAS), ALONG WITH OTHER SMALL APPETIZERS AND DESSERTS, ARE SERVED AT EVERY PARTY YOU ATTEND.

PREP TIME: *10 minutes* | COOKING TIME: *15 minutes* | SERVES: *4–6*

Pasta Frolla (Basic Shortbread) (see recipe on page 153)

½ pound (230g) fresh mozzarella

One 28-ounce (840g) can San Marzano tomatoes

Salt to taste

1 tablespoon (5g) oregano

4 tablespoons (60ml) extra virgin olive oil

Handful arugula for garnish (optional)

INSTRUCTIONS

1. Make the puff pastry, following the recipe on page 153. Roll out the pastry. Once the dough is about ⅛ inch (3mm) thick, cut the dough with a small, round cookie cutter or any other shape you desire. Transfer the cut pieces of dough to a sheet pan lined with parchment paper, leaving 1 inch (2.5cm) (or however much space you think is necessary) between the pieces so that each will bake evenly. Set the tray aside.

2. Cut the fresh mozzarella into small cubes. Drain the excess liquid from the cheese by allowing it to sit in a strainer over a bowl for at least an hour, so when you make your pizza there will be no excess water to make the crust soggy.

3. To prepare the sauce, blend the San Marzano tomatoes with an immersion blender. Add a little salt to taste, the oregano, and olive oil. Use a teaspoon or a pastry bag to place some of the sauce in the middle of each piece of pizza dough and spread it out, leaving roughly ¼ inch (6mm) between the sauce and the edge of the crust. Bake the pizzettas for about 12 minutes at 350°F (180°C) or until the dough has puffed up and is a nice golden brown. Remove the pizzettas from the oven and place a cube of mozzarella on top of each one. Put the pizzettas back in the oven for about 2 minutes. Once the cheese melts, the pizzettas are done. Garnish with some arugula leaves, if you like.

Frittatine Nella Pancetta

(PANCETTA-WRAPPED EGG FRITTATA)

TO GET A GREAT FRITTATA, NEVER BEAT THE EGGS AND THE OTHER INGREDIENTS
TOGETHER. INSTEAD, MIX THEM GENTLY, JUST UNTIL ALL THE INGREDIENTS ARE
COMBINED. IF YOU ARE A VEGETARIAN, YOU CAN SUBSTITUTE SLICED ZUCCHINI FOR
THE PANCETTA, BUT BE SURE TO USE A BAKING CUP, OR LINE YOUR MUFFIN PAN WITH
SOME PARCHMENT PAPER, SO THE ZUCCHINI RETAINS ITS SHAPE.

PREP TIME: *10 minutes* | COOKING TIME: *15 minutes* | SERVES: *4–6 (makes 12 frittatas)*

24 small slices pancetta (or half a
zucchini, cut into thin slices
[for vegetarian option])

5 eggs

⅞ cup (200ml) heavy cream

Salt to taste

¼ onion, chopped fine

3 tablespoons (45g) parmigiano
reggiano, grated

INSTRUCTIONS

1. Place the sliced pancetta in a crisscross pattern, to create a basket to hold the
egg frittata, on a baking sheet. If you are using zucchini instead of pancetta, place
the slices in a muffin mold.

2. In a bowl, whisk the eggs. Add the cream, salt (to taste), chopped onion, and
parmigiano reggiano. Gently mix together all the ingredients. Pour the egg mixture
into the molds, leaving a bit of space at the top to allow room for the mixture to rise.
Preheat the oven to 350°F (180°C) and bake the egg mixture for about 15 minutes or
until the frittatas are done. Let them cool for a couple minutes and then serve.

PRIMI

(FIRST COURSES)

BASED ON TRANSFORMING SIMPLE DISHES INTO TRUE GASTRONOMIC
WONDERS, THE FIRST COURSE IS THE GREAT PRIDE OF ITALIAN CUISINE.
AND, WITHOUT A DOUBT, PASTA IS THE QUEEN OF THE FIRST COURSE.

TAGLIOLINI AL NERO DI SEPPIA CON VONGOLE E RICCI DI MARE *26*

(Squid Ink Tagliolini with Sea Urchin and a Clam and White Wine Sauce)

GNOCCHI DI RICOTTA CON PESTO ALLA GENOVESE *29*

(Ricotta Gnocchi with Genovese Pesto)

GNOCCHI DI PATATE CON SALSA DI POMODORO FRESCO *32*

(Potato Gnocchi with Fresh Tomato Sauce)

TORTELLINI DI CARNE AL BRODO *34*

(Meat Tortellini in Homemade Chicken Broth)

LASAGNA VERDI ALLA BOLOGNESE *38*

(Spinach Lasagna with Meat Sauce)

LASAGNA VEGETARIANA AI CARCIOFINI *42*

(Vegetarian Baby Artichoke Lasagna)

RISOTTO RADICCHIO E GORGONZOLA CON PANCETTA *46*

(Radicchio and Gorgonzola Risotto with Crispy Pancetta)

RISOTTO ASPARAGI *49*

(Asparagus Risotto)

PAPPARDELLE CON RAGU *51*

(Bolognese with Pappardelle)

TAGLIATELLE DI CASTAGNE CON CALABRESE BURRO E SALVIA *53*

*(Chestnut Tagliatelle with Brown Butter Sage Sauce
and Spicy Calabrese Salami)*

Tagliolini al Nero di Seppia con Vongole e Ricci di Mare

(SQUID INK TAGLIOLINI WITH SEA URCHIN AND CLAMS AND WHITE WINE SAUCE)

ONE YEAR, I WENT ON A FAMILY VACATION WITH MY GRANDMA LILIANA AND HER SISTER MAGDA TO A PLACE CALLED SANTA CESAREA TERME IN PUGLIA, IN THE SOUTH OF ITALY. WE WENT TO A RESTAURANT WHERE YOU COULD DIVE AND GET YOUR OWN SEA URCHINS. THEY WOULD THEN COOK WHATEVER YOU BROUGHT UP FROM THE SEA, AND SERVE IT TO YOU WITH SOME FRESH PASTA ON THE SIDE. I REMEMBER THE CHEF JOKINGLY SAYING ABOUT ME, "THIS LITTLE KID BROUGHT UP ENOUGH SEA URCHINS FOR EVERYONE IN THE RESTAURANT TO HAVE SECONDS!"

PREP TIME: *45 minutes* | COOKING TIME: *25 minutes* | SERVES: *4*

FOR THE PASTA

- 2 eggs
- 2 teaspoons (10ml) squid ink (found online and in specialty grocery stores) or kettle fish ink
- 2¾ cups (350g) all-purpose flour

FOR THE CLAM SAUCE

- 2 pounds (1kg) clams, plus more as needed
- 4 tablespoons (60ml) extra virgin olive oil

- 4 cloves garlic
- 1 pinch crushed red pepper
- 1 bunch Italian parsley, minced, plus extra for garnish
- ½ cup (120ml) Pinot Grigio or another dry white wine
- 1 cup (150g) sliced cherry tomatoes
- 12 sea urchins
- Salt and pepper to taste

INSTRUCTIONS

1. To make the pasta: Place the eggs and squid ink in the bowl of a stand mixer, fitted with a dough hook attachment. Add the flour and begin mixing the dough on the lowest speed. Gradually increase the speed to medium-low until it is smooth, occasionally stopping the mixer to pull the dough off the hook, and adding more flour as necessary to keep the dough soft and to keep it from sticking to the dough hook. Take the dough out of the mixer, and, if it is harder than bread dough but still on the soft side, wrap it in plastic wrap and let it rest in the fridge for 30 minutes.

2. Using a rolling pin, roll out the dough into a rectangle, about ½ inch (12mm) thick, and just wide enough to go through a pasta roller. Pass the dough through the roller until the desired thickness is reached.

3. Transfer the dough to a baking sheet or a wooden cutting board lightly dusted with flour to prevent the dough from sticking. Fold the pasta into thirds and use a chef's knife to cut it into ⅛-inch (3mm) wide strips. You can use the fresh pasta right away or freeze it for use later. To cook the pasta, place it in boiling water without any salt, as the squid ink is already salty, for about 3 minutes. Boil frozen or dried pasta for 6–7 minutes.

4. To make the sauce: Rinse the clams under very cold water to remove any sand. Fill a large pot with water and cook the clams over medium heat for 8–10 minutes with the lid on, until they fully open. Discard any clams that do not open. The liquid produced by cooking the clams is the most important part of the sauce. Using a chinois (a cone-shaped sieve with a closely woven mesh) or a cheesecloth over a large bowl, strain the liquid from the clams to remove any sand. Set the bowl aside and reserve the clam juice.

5. In a large nonstick pan, place all the oil, garlic, crushed red pepper, and minced parsley, and cook over medium heat until the garlic just begins to turn golden. Take the pan off the stove and deglaze it by adding a little bit of wine to cook off the alcohol. Put the pan back on the stove. Add the reserved clam juice and cherry tomatoes and let the mixture reduce for roughly 15 minutes. Once it is reduced, add the clams and pasta.

6. Assembly: Toss everything together and plate it. Finish by garnishing the dish with some fresh sea urchins. Sprinkle a bit of fresh chopped parsley on top. *Buon Appetito.*

Gnocchi di Ricotta con Pesto alla Genovese

(RICOTTA GNOCCHI WITH GENOVESE PESTO)

WHEN YOU COME HOME FROM WORK AND HAVE NO TIME TO BOIL POTATOES, THE SOLUTION IS TO WHIP UP FRESH GNOCCHI. WHAT'S BETTER THAN THAT? WHEN I WAS A CHILD, MY FATHER TAUGHT ME HOW TO CREATE THIS FAST, FRESH, EASY-TO-MAKE, DELICIOUS GNOCCHI COMBINED WITH HOMEMADE PESTO. IT'S A PERFECT FAMILY DINNER THAT ANYONE CAN MAKE. IT GOES WELL WITH MANY DIFFERENT SUMMER SAUCES, LIKE A NICE SAN MARZANO TOMATO SAUCE, A SICILIAN PESTO SAUCE, AND, OF COURSE, GENOVESE PESTO, LIKE THE ONE IN THIS RECIPE.

PREP TIME: *20 minutes* | COOKING TIME: *5 minutes* | SERVES: *4–6*

FOR THE GNOCCHI

- 15 ounces (500g) ricotta cheese
- Zest of 1 lemon
- Pinch of salt
- 1 ½ cups (130g) parmigiano, grated
- 2 eggs
- 1 ¾ cups (220g) all-purpose flour
- Pinch of ground nutmeg

FOR THE PESTO

- 3½ ounces (100g) fresh basil leaves
- 1 clove garlic
- 1 ¼ cups (100g) parmigiano, grated
- Juice of 1 lemon
- Pinch of salt and pepper
- ¼ cup (30g) pine nuts
- 1¼ cups (300ml) extra virgin olive oil
- Handful of basil leaves, sliced

INSTRUCTIONS

1. To make the gnocchi: Put the ricotta in a bowl, and then add the lemon zest, salt, grated parmigiano, eggs, and flour. Use a wooden spoon to mix everything together until the mixture is well combined. Sprinkle some flour on a clean, smooth surface and remove a piece of the gnocchi dough from the bowl. The dough should be as big as your hand can roll it. Roll it out until it is about ½ inch to ¾ inch (12–20mm) thick. With a knife, cut the dough into ½-inch (12mm) pieces to make the gnocchi.

2. To make the pesto: Place the basil leaves, garlic, parmigiano, lemon juice, pinch of salt, pinch of pepper, and all of the pine nuts except for a small handful

for garnishing into a food processor. Start blending and slowly pour in all of the olive oil except for a tablespoon (5g) until the sauce is well combined and has a creamy consistency. This is a very simple sauce to make if you have a food processor, but the people from Genova still believe that real pesto must be made by hand, using a mortar and pestle, to really get the full depth of flavor from this amazing traditional sauce.

3. Cook the gnocchi in hot boiling water with some salt. Add some extra virgin olive oil to prevent the gnocchi from sticking together. Boil the gnocchi for about 5 minutes. Remove the gnocchi from the water and put them in a bowl with the fresh pesto and gently mix them together. Plate the gnocchi and top with some parmigiano, sliced basil leaves, and a sprinkle of pine nuts.

Gnocchi di Patate con Salsa di Pomodoro Fresco

(POTATO GNOCCHI WITH FRESH TOMATO SAUCE)

THIS RECIPE IS ONE OF MY FAVORITES BECAUSE YOU CAN TASTE ALL THE FLAVORS OF ITALY IN JUST ONE DISH. IT REPRESENTS EVERYTHING THAT I LOVE ABOUT TRADITIONAL ITALIAN COOKING. THE ONIONS, TOMATOES, AND BASIL ALL COME FROM THE SAME GARDEN, AND, ALONG WITH THE SOFT TEXTURE OF THE GNOCCHI, THE RESULTING DISH IS DEEPLY FAMILIAR TO EVERY ITALIAN.

PREP TIME: *25 minutes* | COOKING TIME: *35 minutes* | SERVES: *4–6*

FOR THE GNOCCHI

3 potatoes

Salt and pepper to taste

Parmigiano, grated

2 eggs

1 cup (125g) all-purpose flour

Extra virgin olive oil, for cooking water

1 spoonful fresh ricotta or grated ricotta salata, for garnish

FOR THE SAUCE

4 tablespoons (60ml) extra virgin olive oil

1 peperoncino (or Fresno chili), with the seeds scraped out and sliced

1 onion, chopped

2–3 heirloom tomatoes, chopped

2 garlic cloves, crushed

16 fresh basil leaves, plus some for garnish

Salt and pepper to taste

INSTRUCTIONS

1. To make the gnocchi: Wash, boil, and peel the potatoes, once they're cool. Put the potatoes in a stand mixer, fitted with a paddle attachment, and mash them thoroughly. Add the salt and pepper to taste, the eggs, and flour. Mix until well combined. Place dough on a lightly floured surface. Take a small piece of the dough and roll it out until it is a ½–¾ inch (12–20mm), like a thin dowel or a long log. Then with a knife cut the dough into ½-inch (12mm) pieces and give a slight pinch, creating little square pillows.

2. To make the sauce: Place the olive oil, sliced peperoncino, and onion in a small saucepan. Cook the mixture until the onion is golden. Add the chopped fresh tomatoes, garlic, basil leaves, and salt and pepper to taste, and cook for about 15 minutes until the tomatoes reduce to a sauce.

3. Cook the gnocchi for about 5 minutes in boiling water with some salt and add a little extra virgin olive oil to prevent the gnocchi from sticking together. Remove the gnocchi from the water and add it to the pan with the fresh tomato sauce. Cook the sauce for another 2 minutes and then plate it.

4. Sprinkle some fresh ricotta or grate some ricotta salata over the gnocchi. Garnish with a basil leaf.

Tortellini di Carne al Brodo

(MEAT TORTELLINI IN HOMEMADE CHICKEN BROTH)

THIS IS MY GRANDMA ROSITA'S FAVORITE DISH. SHE RAISED HENS AND WOULD SEND MY BROTHER AND ME TO FETCH FRESH EGGS EVERY MORNING FROM THE HENHOUSE. ON COLD AND RAINY DAYS, SHE WOULD INVITE US TO COME OVER AND HELP MAKE TORTELLINI, ALWAYS MADE FROM SCRATCH, FOR MY GRANDPA ROMANO, USING THE SAME FRESH EGGS THAT MY BROTHER AND I COLLECTED THAT MORNING. THEN WE WOULD ALL SIT DOWN TOGETHER AND EAT IT, LAUGHING AND ENJOYING THE TIME WE HAD TOGETHER.

PREP TIME: *75 minutes* | COOKING TIME: *70 minutes* | SERVES: *4–6*

FOR THE CHICKEN BROTH

- 1 whole chicken (approximately 4 pounds [2kg])
- 2 carrots, chopped into large pieces
- 2 celery stalks, chopped into large pieces
- 2 onions, chopped into large pieces
- 2 garlic cloves
- 2 bay leaves
- Salt, to taste
- Freshly ground pepper, to taste

FOR THE FILLING

- 3 tablespoons (45ml) extra virgin olive oil
- ⅓ pound (150g) ground beef, 2% fat
- Salt and pepper to taste
- ⅓ pound (150g) ground pork
- ¹⁄₁₀ pound (50g) ground mortadella
- ½ cup (40g) parmigiano, grated, plus some shaved for garnish
- 1 cup (100g) bread crumbs
- 2 eggs
- 1 teaspoon (2.5g) ground nutmeg
- 1 small bunch chopped parsley
- 1 teaspoon (2.5g) fresh thyme (leaves only)

FOR THE PASTA

- 3 cups (360g) all-purpose flour, plus more as needed
- 4 eggs + 1 egg yolk

INSTRUCTIONS

1. To make the chicken broth: First, clean the chicken by running it under some cold water. Put it in a large stockpot with the vegetables and the bay leaves. Add enough water to cover the chicken, vegetables, and bay leaves. Cover the pot with a tight-fitting lid and cook on medium-low heat for at least 50 minutes to 1 hour. Every 10 minutes, remove any foam that rises to the top of the pot. Removing the foam will give you a clear broth and improve the flavor.

2. Once the broth is ready, strain the broth through a chinois (a conical sieve with an extremely fine mesh) or cheesecloth to remove any leftover foam, then let the broth cool. Once the broth starts to cool, the fat from the chicken will slowly rise to the top and create a clear film. Use a ladle to remove this film every 10–15 minutes. When there is no longer any fat settling at the top, the broth is ready. Taste it and add a little salt and pepper, if needed.

3. To make the filling: While the broth is cooking, start making the meat filling. Heat 3 tablespoons (45ml) of the olive oil in a saucepan, and then add the ground beef and pork. Season the meat with a little salt and pepper. Cook the mixture for about 10 minutes over medium heat, moving it around to make sure it cooks thoroughly.

4. Once the meat is cooked, add the mortadella to the mix and use a food processor to grind the meat one more time. The meat filling for this recipe needs to be ground as finely as possible. Put the ground meat in a large bowl and add the rest of the filling ingredients—the parmigiano, bread crumbs, eggs, nutmeg, and herbs—and mix until all are combined. Set the mixture aside.

5. To make the pasta: Place the flour and eggs in the bowl of a stand mixer, fitted with a hook attachment, and mix until the ingredients have combined into a dough. The pasta dough is ready when it no longer sticks to the hook attachment and comes off the sides of the bowl easily. Wrap the dough in plastic wrap and let it rest in the fridge for 30 minutes.

6. To make the tortellini, lay the pasta dough on a smooth, clean surface. Sprinkle some flour over your working station and on top of the pasta dough to prevent it from sticking to the surface. Use a rolling pin to make the dough ⅛-inch (3mm) thick.

7. Cut the dough into approximately 3-inch (8cm) squares, then fill the center of each square with a teaspoon (5ml) of the filling. Fold the square into a triangle and then pinch the corners. Fold the widest part of the triangle toward the filling and then pinch the other 2 corners together to make a tortellini shape. You can freeze any tortellini that you don't use for up to 2 months in a freezer bag.

8. When the broth is ready, bring it to a boil, and then reduce the heat to medium (so that your tortellini do not break open when they hit the water). Add the tortellini and cook them for 3–4 minutes. You'll know they're done when they start to float to the top.

9. Serve the tortellini in a bowl with some broth. Garnish with some freshly shaved parmigiano and enjoy.

Lasagna Verdi alla Bolognese

(SPINACH LASAGNA WITH MEAT SAUCE)

I OWE MOST OF MY PASTA-MAKING SKILLS TO MY GRANDMA ROSITA. MY GRANDPARENTS LIVED IN A SMALL TOWN NEAR BOLOGNA, WHERE THERE WEREN'T VERY MANY OTHER CHILDREN MY AGE TO PLAY WITH. EACH TIME I WENT TO STAY WITH MY GRANDPARENTS, I WOULD END UP HELPING GRANDMA ROSITA MAKE ALL KINDS OF DIFFERENT PASTAS, BUT MY ALL-TIME FAVORITE WAS LASAGNA. HER SECRET RECIPE INCLUDED A BÉCHAMEL SAUCE THAT WAS RICH AND CREAMY, WITH A DELICIOUS AROMA OF FRESH NUTMEG AND THYME. JUST THINKING ABOUT IT NOW MAKES MY MOUTH WATER.

PREP TIME: *90 minutes* | COOKING TIME: *4½ hours* | SERVES: *4–6*

FOR THE PASTA

2 ounces (60g) spinach

Pinch of salt

3 eggs

2¼ cups (300g) all-purpose flour, plus more for dusting

FOR THE BOLOGNESE SAUCE

2 carrots

2 celery stalks

2 onions

1 cup (240ml) extra virgin olive oil

1 teaspoon (5ml) crushed red pepper

1 pound (450g) ground beef

1¼ cups (300ml) red wine

1 tablespoon (15ml) tomato paste

One 15-ounce (400g) can chopped tomatoes, reserving the juice

1 tablespoon (5g) nutmeg

8–10 sprigs fresh thyme

Salt and pepper to taste

FOR THE BÉCHAMEL SAUCE

1 quart (1L) whole milk

7 tablespoons (0.22 pound [100g]) butter

½ cup (60g) all-purpose flour

1 pinch ground nutmeg

Salt to taste

FOR THE ASSEMBLY

2 cups (300g) parmigiano, grated

INSTRUCTIONS

1. To make the pasta: Start by rinsing the spinach in some cold water. Fill a large pot with water and boil the spinach with a little salt. Once it is cooked, remove the spinach

from the hot water and let it drain through a colander. For the best results, wait until the spinach is cool and squeeze out as much excess water as possible by hand.

2. Using a food processor, chop the spinach until it has a creamy consistency. Put it in a bowl, and add the eggs and flour. Use a handheld mixer to mix everything together until you have a nice soft ball of dough. Wrap it up and let it rest in the fridge for 30 minutes.

3. Sprinkle some flour on a large cutting board or kitchen counter and pinch off a piece of the pasta dough as big as your fist. Using a rolling pin, roll the dough until it is very thin (approximately ⅛ inch [3mm] thick) and cut off strips that are as long as your lasagna pan (you want to make sure they fit in the pan).

4. To make the Bolognese sauce: While the dough is resting, start making the Bolognese sauce. Finely chop the carrots, celery, and onions. Place all the olive oil in a stockpot over medium heat and cook the carrots, celery, and onions for about 7–8 minutes. Add the crushed red pepper and continue to cook until the onion is golden. Finally, add the ground beef and cook the mixture for another 3 minutes.

5. Keep cooking the meat and vegetables until they start to stick to the bottom of the pot and begin to caramelize, but don't let them burn. This caramelization will help give the sauce its great flavor. Once the mixture is caramelized, pour in the wine and keep stirring it until it evaporates. The wine will take away any remaining odor of fat from the meat. Deglaze the pot by scraping the bottom and then adding the tomato paste, the chopped tomatoes and their juice, nutmeg, fresh thyme, and the salt and pepper to taste. Remember that the star of a classic Italian Bolognese sauce is the meat, not the tomatoes, so do not add any extra tomatoes.

6. Cook the Bolognese sauce over low heat and let it simmer for at least 1½ hours, or until the olive oil starts to separate and float to the top. This is a sign that your sauce is done.

7. To make the béchamel sauce: In a heavy-bottomed or nonstick saucepan, start heating the milk, bringing it just to a boil. While it is heating, use another nonstick pan to melt the butter. When it has melted, take the pan off the heat and add the flour, a little bit at a time, to create a roux (a mixture of flour and butter). Put the pan back on medium heat and keep stirring the roux until it gets a little color. Use a whisk to continuously stir the

roux, while you slowly add the hot milk. When the flour, milk, and butter mixture starts to boil, it will begin to thicken.

8. Take the béchamel off the heat and finish it by adding the nutmeg and salt to taste.

9. Preheat the oven to 350°F (180°C).

10. Assembly: Spread a layer of béchamel on the bottom of a casserole or baking dish. Next, place a layer of the Bolognese sauce and the grated parmigiano. Lay a sheet of pasta over the sauce. Continue to layer the béchamel, Bolognese sauce, parmigiano, and pasta until you have 4–5 layers. Finish the top layer with grated parmigiano.

11. Cover the casserole or baking dish with aluminum foil and cook the lasagna for about 30 minutes. After 30 minutes, remove the foil and let the lasagna continue to bake for 10–15 minutes more, or until the cheese on top starts to brown.

12. Remove the lasagna from the oven and let it sit for 5 minutes before serving. Garnish the lasagna with some freshly chopped parsley, if you like.

Lasagna Vegetariana ai Carciofini

(VEGETARIAN BABY ARTICHOKE LASAGNA)

I WOULD HAVE TO SAY THAT I LOVE TO EAT MEAT, BUT I LOVE VEGETABLES JUST AS MUCH, IF NOT MORE SO. MY COUSINS CHIARA AND MARTINA GREW UP AS VEGETARIANS AND PROTESTED AGAINST ALL THE MEAT DISHES THAT WERE SERVED AT EVERY FAMILY GATHERING. I, ON THE OTHER HAND, WAS ALL FOR MEAT—JUST TO ANTAGONIZE THEM. MY AUNT LUANA ALWAYS MADE A FABULOUS VEGETARIAN LASAGNA JUST FOR THEM. I WOULD SPEND MOST OF MY TIME TEASING MY COUSINS FOR MISSING OUT ON SO MUCH DELICIOUS FOOD, BUT THEN, WHEN THEY WEREN'T LOOKING, I WOULD HELP MYSELF TO A LARGE PIECE OF THEIR SPECIAL LASAGNA.

PREP TIME: *75 minutes* | COOKING TIME: *75 minutes* | SERVES: *4–6*

FOR THE PASTA

2 ¼ cups (300g) flour

3 eggs

FOR THE ARTICHOKE SAUCE

5 pounds (2kg) baby artichokes

5 tablespoons (75ml) extra virgin olive oil

2 onions, chopped

Salt and pepper to taste

½ cup (120ml) white wine

1 tablespoon (15ml) tomato paste

One 15-ounce (400g) can diced tomatoes, reserving the juice

FOR THE BÉCHAMEL SAUCE

1 quart (1L) whole milk

7 tablespoons (0.22 pound [100g]) butter

½ cup (60g) all-purpose flour

1 pinch ground nutmeg

Salt to taste

INSTRUCTIONS

1. To make the pasta: In a bowl, mix the flour with the eggs, using a hand mixer, or just a fork and then your hands to combine them, until the dough holds together enough for you to work it with your hands. Continue to work the dough until you can form it into a soft ball. Wrap the dough in plastic wrap and let it rest in the fridge for 30 minutes.

2. After 30 minutes, take the dough out of the fridge. Sprinkle some flour on a large cutting board or kitchen counter and pinch off a fist-size piece of the pasta dough. Using a rolling pin, roll the dough until it is very thin, about ⅛-inch (3mm) thick, and

cut off strips that are as long as your lasagna pan (you want to make sure they fit in the pan). Cook the pasta in batches (2–3 strips at a time) in a large pot of boiling water for about 3 minutes. Drain the pasta and let it cool on kitchen towels.

3. To make the artichoke sauce: While the dough is resting, start making the artichoke sauce. Clean the artichokes by removing the outer leaves until you reach the heart of the artichoke. Cut the artichoke heart in half, remove the hair in the center, and clean the stem. Cook the artichokes in boiling water for at least 12 minutes until they are soft. Next, cut the artichokes into julienne slices. (See the box on page 45 for instructions on trimming and preparing artichokes.)

4. If you're not making the sauce right away, be sure to put the artichokes in a bowl with cold water and lemon juice to keep them from turning brown.

5. In a large sauté pan, heat up the extra virgin olive oil and add the chopped onions. Cook the onions about 6–7 minutes on medium heat with some salt and pepper until the onions are translucent. Add the artichokes and sauté them with the onions for about 5 minutes. Be sure to move them back and forth constantly to keep them from burning.

6. Take the pan off the stove and deglaze it by adding about a half cup (120ml) of the white wine, quickly moving everything back and forth in the pan, and tossing the food slightly in the air. This will help cook out the alcohol.

7. Finally, add the tomato paste, the diced tomatoes and their juice, and cook the sauce for 30–40 minutes on medium-low heat. It is done once it starts to thicken. Finish the sauce by adding some fresh basil leaves.

8. Make the béchamel sauce (pages 40–41, Step 7 and Step 8).

9. Assembly: Spread a layer of béchamel around the bottom of a casserole or baking dish. Next, spread a layer of the artichoke sauce, then the parmigiano, and finally a layer of pasta. Repeat this process until you have at least 4–5 layers. The final layer should be pasta, artichoke sauce, béchamel, and then parmigiano. Cover the casserole or baking dish with foil and bake the lasagna for about 20 minutes at 350°F (180°C). Remove the foil and continue to bake the lasagna for another 10–15 minutes and voilà—it's hot and ready to serve!

HOW TO TRIM
AND PREPARE AN ARTICHOKE

a) Remove the tough outer leaves until you see the pale yellow ones. **b)** Trim the leaves that cover the base of the heart. **c)** Remove half of the stem and clean the remaining half with a knife. **d)** Chop off the top of the artichoke and slice it in half. **e)** Use a spoon to remove the fibrous part of the artichoke. **f)** Slice thinly.

Risotto Radicchio e Gorgonzola con Pancetta

(RADICCHIO AND GORGONZOLA RISOTTO WITH CRISPY PANCETTA)

ALTHOUGH MOST PEOPLE DON'T EXPERIENCE THEIR FIRST TASTE OF RADICCHIO UNTIL THEY'RE GROWN-UPS, I HAVE ENJOYED ITS DELICIOUS BITTER TASTE SINCE I WAS LITTLE. SWEET GORGONZOLA, MIXED IN WITH RADICCHIO, CREATES A DELICIOUS BALANCE OF FLAVORS. THIS RECIPE IS A GREAT METAPHOR FOR LIFE: THERE ARE SWEET MOMENTS AND BITTER ONES, BUT YOU HAVE TO HAVE BOTH IN ORDER TO APPRECIATE HOW GREAT THE GOOD ONES ARE.

PREP TIME: *10 minutes* | COOKING TIME: *25–30 minutes* | SERVES: *4*

4 tablespoons (60ml) extra virgin olive oil, plus extra for frying pancetta

2 shallots, diced

2 cups (400g) Arborio rice

½ cup (120ml) white wine, such as Pinot Grigio

1½ quarts (1.5L) chicken broth

5 ounces (140g) diced pancetta

½ cup (120ml) heavy cream

⅓ cup (50g) Gorgonzola cheese, crumbled

1 bunch radicchio, coarsely chopped

½ cup (40g) parmigiano, grated

Salt and pepper to taste

INSTRUCTIONS

1. In a saucepan, heat all the olive oil. Add the shallots and cook them until they are golden (for approximately 4–5 minutes). When the shallots are done, add the Arborio rice and keep stirring the mixture 2–3 minutes longer to lightly toast the rice. This will help release its fragrant aroma.

2. Add the white wine and cook until it all evaporates. Start adding just enough of the chicken broth to cover the rice and continue to let it simmer on low heat. Make sure to constantly stir and check the rice to keep it from burning. Once the rice has absorbed all the broth, add more. Continue this process for 15–20 minutes or until the rice is almost al dente. Make sure not to overcook the rice.

3. While you are waiting for the rice to cook, start making the crispy pancetta. Heat a splash of extra virgin olive oil in a small pan, and then toss in the diced pancetta. Move the pancetta back and forth in the pan until it has cooked and is nice and crispy. This process should take 4–5 minutes. When the pancetta is done, remove it from the pan and let it sit on a plate lined with paper towels to soak up the excess fat and keep the pancetta from getting soggy.

4. When the rice is almost al dente, start adding the cream, Gorgonzola, and radicchio. Mix everything together, and then add the parmigiano. Cook the risotto for another 2–3 minutes. Add salt and pepper to taste.

5. Plate and garnish the risotto with the crispy pancetta and serve immediately.

Risotto Asparagi

(ASPARAGUS RISOTTO)

IF YOU WANT A REALLY GOOD VEGETARIAN RISOTTO, THIS ONE IS SUPER FRESH WITH A TOUCH OF SWEETNESS FROM THE SHALLOTS.

PREP TIME: *15 minutes* | COOKING TIME: *55 minutes* | SERVES: *4*

INGREDIENTS

1 bunch (10–15 ounces [300–400g]) asparagus

4 tablespoons (60ml) extra virgin olive oil, plus more for sautéing the asparagus heads

2 shallots, chopped and divided

2 cups (400g) Arborio rice

½ cup (120ml) white wine

1½ quarts (1.5L) vegetable broth

¼ cup (60ml) heavy cream or 7 tablespoons (100g) butter

½ cup (40g) parmigiano, grated, for the topping

2 garlic cloves, crushed

Salt and pepper to taste

INSTRUCTIONS

1. Chop off just the heads of the asparagus and set them aside. Chop the rest of the asparagus into pieces and cook them in boiling water for 5 minutes. Drain and set them aside.

2. In a pan, heat half the olive oil, then add half of the chopped shallots and the parboiled asparagus. Cook the asparagus until it is tender, about 5–8 minutes. Remove the shallot-and-asparagus mixture from the pan and use a handheld blender or an immersion blender to purée it. Pass the purée through a fine mesh strainer to remove any excess pieces of asparagus. In the same pan, heat the remaining olive oil and cook the remaining chopped shallots until they're golden.

3. Add the Arborio rice to a large pan and keep stirring it for 2–3 minutes to lightly toast the rice. This will help release its fragrant aroma. Add the white wine to the pan and cook until it evaporates. Start adding just enough of the vegetable broth to cover the rice and let it continue to simmer on low heat. Make sure to constantly stir and check on the rice to keep it from burning. Once the rice has absorbed the broth, add more. Continue this process for 15–20 minutes or until the rice is almost al dente. Make sure not to overcook the rice.

4. When the rice is almost al dente, start adding the cream or butter and the asparagus purée. Mix everything together and then add the parmigiano. Cook the rice for another 2–3 minutes. Meanwhile, sauté the asparagus heads in a small pan with a little olive oil and the crushed garlic until the heads are browned and crispy.

5. Plate the risotto with the crispy asparagus heads on top as a garnish, and to give the dish a nice crunch. Add salt and pepper to taste. Serve immediately.

Pappardelle con Ragu

(BOLOGNESE SAUCE WITH PAPPARDELLE)

THIS IS A CLASSIC BOLOGNESE DISH THAT I SAVORED AT OUR MOUNTAIN HOME IN PIANACCIO.

PREP TIME: *60 minutes* | COOKING TIME: *2 hours* | SERVES: *4–6*

FOR THE DOUGH

4½ cups (550g) flour, plus more for dusting

4 eggs

FOR THE BOLOGNESE SAUCE

2 carrots

2 celery stalks

2 onions

1 cup (240ml) extra virgin olive oil

1 teaspoon (5ml) crushed red pepper

1 pound (500g) ground beef

1¼ cups (300ml) red wine

1 tablespoon (15ml) tomato paste

One 15-ounce (400g) can chopped tomatoes, reserving the juice

1 tablespoon (5g) nutmeg

8–10 sprigs fresh thyme

Salt and pepper to taste

INSTRUCTIONS

1. To make the dough: In a bowl, mix the flour with the eggs, using a hand mixer, or just a fork and then your hands to combine them, until the dough holds together enough for you to work it with your hands. Continue to work the dough until you can form it into a soft ball. Wrap the dough in plastic wrap and let it rest in the fridge for 30 minutes.

2. After 30 minutes, take the dough out of the fridge. Sprinkle some flour on a large cutting board or kitchen counter and pinch off a piece of the pasta dough. Using a rolling pin, roll the dough until it is very thin and cut it into long pieces, about ½ inch (12mm) wide.

3. To make the sauce: While the dough is resting, start making the Bolognese sauce. Finely chop the carrots, celery, and onions. In a large stockpot, heat the olive oil over medium heat, and cook the carrots, celery, and onions. Add the crushed red pepper and continue to cook the mixture for about 4–5 minutes until the onion is golden. Finally, add the ground beef.

4. Keep cooking the meat and vegetables for at least 10–15 minutes until they start to stick to the bottom of the pot and begin to caramelize, but don't let them burn. This caramelization will help flavor the sauce. Once the mixture has caramelized, pour in the red wine and keep stirring the pot until the alcohol has evaporated. The wine will take away any remaining odor of fat from the meat. Deglaze the pot by scraping the bottom. When it is deglazed, add the tomato paste, chopped tomatoes, nutmeg, fresh thyme, and salt and pepper to taste. Remember that the star of a classic Italian Bolognese sauce is the meat, not the tomatoes, so do not add extra tomatoes.

5. Cook the sauce on low heat and let it simmer for at least 1½ hours or until the olive oil starts to separate and float to the top. This is a sign that the sauce is done.

6. Cook the pasta in boiling water until it is al dente, after about 2–3 minutes in the boiling water, and then mix it into the sauce in the stockpot.

Tagliatelle di Castagne con Calabrese Burro e Salvia

(CHESTNUT TAGLIATELLE WITH BROWN BUTTER SAGE SAUCE AND SPICY CALABRESE SALAMI)

I CREATED THIS RECIPE AS A SPECIAL DISH FOR ONE OF MY CARRARA FOOD AND PASTRY SHOPS IN CALIFORNIA. IT WAS INSPIRED BY MEMORIES OF PICKING CHESTNUTS WITH MY GRANDPA, AND MAKING THEM INTO FRESH CHESTNUT FLOUR PASTA.

PREP TIME: *40 minutes*　|　COOKING TIME: *20 minutes*　|　SERVES: *4*

1 cup (100g) chestnut flour

2 cups (200g) all-purpose flour, plus more for dusting

3 eggs

8 tablespoons (110g) butter

16 sage leaves

About 12 slices salami

Salt and pepper to taste

INSTRUCTIONS

1. In a bowl, mix the flours with the eggs, using a fork or a handheld mixer to combine them, until the dough holds together enough for you to work it with your hands. Continue to work the dough until you can form it into a soft ball. Wrap the dough in plastic wrap and let it rest in the fridge for 30 minutes.

2. After 30 minutes, take it out of the fridge. Sprinkle some flour on a large cutting board or kitchen counter and pinch off a fist-size piece of the pasta dough. Using a rolling pin, roll the dough until it is very thin (about ⅛-inch-[3mm] thick,) and cut it into long, ¼-inch (6mm) wide strips. Cook the pasta in boiling water until it is al dente, for about 2–3 minutes.

3. Next, add the butter to a medium saucepan. When it begins to melt, add the sage and salami. Let it cook until the butter turns slightly brown and the sage and salami are crispy. Add the cooked pasta to the pan and mix it in with the sauce. Season with salt and pepper to taste.

SECONDI
(MAIN COURSES)

THE DISHES YOU PREPARE FOR THE MAIN COURSE SHOULD ALLOW YOU TO UNLEASH YOUR IMAGINATION AND GIVE YOU THE FREEDOM TO INNOVATE WITH A WIDE VARIETY OF INGREDIENTS AND ENDLESS COMBINATIONS OF FLAVORS AND TEXTURES. WHETHER THE MAIN COURSE FOCUSES ON MEAT, FISH, VEGETABLES, OR A VEGETARIAN DISH, THE ULTIMATE GOAL IS ALWAYS TO IMPRESS WITH A SOPHISTICATED, HARMONIOUS BLEND OF INGREDIENTS, AND A DELICATE CONTRAST OF FLAVORS THAT MAKE EVEN THE MOST SIMPLE DISH SPECIAL.

FILETTO AL PEPE VERDE CON FUNGHI PORCINI   *56*

(Green Peppercorn Filet Mignon with Porcini Mushrooms)

BISTECCA ALLA FIORENTINA CON ASPARAGI, CAROTE E CARCIOFI   *59*

(Porterhouse Steak with Asparagus, Carrots, and Artichokes)

COSCIE DI RANA SALTIMBOCCA CON CAVOLINI DI BRUXELLES   *60*

(Frogs' Legs Saltimbocca with Brussels Sprouts)

FILETTO DI MAIOLE CON SALSA AL LATTE   *63*

(Pork Tenderloin with Milk Sauce)

BRANZINO ALLA ERBE IN CROSTA DI SALE   *65*

(Salt-Encrusted Sea Bass)

FILETTO DI BRANZINO CON TESTE DI ASPARAGI E PURÉE DI CAVOLFIORE   *68*

(Sea Bass Filet with Asparagus Tips and Cauliflower Purée)

PESCE SPADA CON INSALATA E NOCI PECAN   *70*

(Swordfish with Butter Lettuce and Pecans)

POLLO ALLA MILANESE CON PORCINI FRITTI E RUCOLA   *72*

(Chicken Milanese with Fried Porcini Mushrooms and Arugula Salad)

POLLO BURRO E SALVIA CON PATATE ARROSTITE IN PADELLA   *75*

(Brown Butter Sage Chicken with Fingerling Potatoes)

MY FATHER'S ROAST BEEF   *77*

Filetto al Pepe Verde con Funghi Porcini

(GREEN PEPPERCORN FILET MIGNON WITH PORCINI MUSHROOMS)

A GOOD STEAK NEEDS VERY LITTLE PREPARATION AND VERY LITTLE SEASONING. AT LEAST ONCE A WEEK, FOR DINNER, I HAVE A NICE PIECE OF STEAK, PERFECTLY COOKED RARE TO MEDIUM RARE, WITH A BIT OF SALT AND PEPPER AND FINISHED WITH SOME VERY GOOD OLIVE OIL. BUT WHEN I SERVE A STEAK, WITH A DELICIOUS SIDE DISH OF PORCINI MUSHROOMS, I LIKE TO CREATE A SAUCE THAT WILL COMPLEMENT IT. PORCINI MUSHROOMS ARE VERY MEATY, AND PAIRING THEM WITH A PEPPERCORN CREAM SAUCE BRINGS OUT THE MUSHROOMS' NATURALLY WOODY AND NUTTY FLAVORS.

PREP TIME: *5 minutes* | COOKING TIME: *40 minutes* | SERVES: *2*

INGREDIENTS

- ½ pound (230g) filet mignon
- Salt and pepper to taste
- 4 tablespoons (60g) butter
- ¼ cup (60ml) cognac or brandy
- ½–1 cup (40–80g) green peppercorns
- ½ cup (120ml) heavy cream

- 4–6 tablespoons (60–80g) extra virgin olive oil
- 3 cloves garlic, crushed
- 1 small bunch fresh Italian parsley
- 1 teaspoon (2.5g) crushed red pepper
- ½ pound (230g) porcini mushrooms, thinly sliced
- 1 tablespoon (16g) tomato paste

INSTRUCTIONS

1. Start by slicing the filet mignon into three 1½-inch (4cm) thick pieces. Take a piece of twine and wrap it around each slice of meat. This will keep the filet mignon tender after cooking. Salt and pepper the filet mignon. In a nonstick pan, melt the butter and sear the filet on each side on medium to high heat for 2 minutes. Take the filet off the heat before adding the brandy or cognac. Please use extreme caution here. Keep in mind that when cognac or brandy is added to a very hot pan, it may quickly burst into flames, so have a large lid ready to cover the pan, in case the liquor catches fire. Be very careful, and once the alcohol is cooked off, put the pan back on the stove. This will cook off any odor of fat and also release the beautiful aroma of the meat.

2. Cook the filet for 3–4 minutes more on each side, over medium to high heat. Transfer the meat from the pan to a plate and place the peppercorns and cream in the pan. Reduce the mixture until it thickens and becomes a sauce. Put the filet back in the pan with the sauce, turning over the meat for about 1 minute on each side to let it absorb the flavors of the sauce.

3. Preheat the oven to 375°F (190°C).

4. Remove the meat from the pan once again and place it in an ovenproof dish. Put the dish in the oven and cook it at 375°F (190°C) for about 5 minutes, if you want it cooked medium rare. Cook the filet an additional 3 minutes for medium, and 6 minutes for medium-well to well done. Take the filet out of the oven and remove the twine. Let the meat rest for 5 minutes before plating and pouring the sauce on top.

5. To make the mushrooms, heat about 2–3 tablespoons (30–40g) extra virgin olive oil in a small saucepan and add the garlic, parsley, and red pepper. Sauté the mushrooms for 1 minute and then add some porcini mushrooms and the tomato paste. Season the mushrooms with salt and pepper, and then cover the pan with a lid. Stir the mushrooms every few minutes. After 12–15 minutes, remove the lid and cook the mushroom for 3–4 more minutes. The mushrooms will release water, once they start cooking, so make sure to cook off all the liquid.

6. Finally, plate the filet mignon with the cream sauce and the porcini mushrooms on top.

Bistecca alla Fiorentina con Asparagi, Carote e Carciofi

(PORTERHOUSE STEAK WITH ASPARAGUS, CARROTS, AND ARTICHOKES)

BISTECCA ALLA FIORENTINA IS ONE OF THE MOST POPULAR STEAKS IN ITALY. MY DAD USED TO MAKE THIS DISH ON A WOOD-FIRE GRILL THAT HE AND MY GRANDPA BUILT. EVERY SUMMER, MY FRIENDS AND I WOULD GET TOGETHER AND HELP MY DAD GRILL THESE DELICIOUS STEAKS.

PREP TIME: *10–15 minutes* | COOKING TIME: *45 minutes* | SERVES: *2–4*

Two 1-pound (500g) porterhouse steaks

½ cup (120ml), plus 2 tablespoons (30ml) extra virgin olive oil, and more for drizzling

Salt and pepper to taste

3 rosemary sprigs, chopped

2 thyme sprigs, chopped

8 sage leaves, chopped

1 carrot

1¼ pounds (550g) asparagus

5 baby artichokes

3 garlic cloves, crushed

INSTRUCTIONS

1. Marinate the steaks in ½ cup (120ml) of the olive oil, the salt and pepper, and the chopped rosemary, thyme, and sage. Let the steaks sit in the marinade for about 30 minutes.

2. In the meantime, wash the vegetables. Dry them off after you wash them. Transfer the vegetables to a cutting board and use a chef's knife to julienne the vegetables (i.e., cut the vegetables into long, matchstick-thin strips). To clean and trim the artichokes, see sidebar on page 45.

3. In a nonstick pan, heat up 2 tablespoons of olive oil, the crushed garlic, and all the vegetables. Sauté them for about 7–8 minutes until everything starts to get crisp. Lower the heat to medium, letting the vegetables sit for approximately 10–15 minutes so they get crispy without burning.

4. On a grill, start cooking the steaks over high heat. Let the steaks cook for about 5–7 minutes on each side, making sure you get nice grill marks without burning the meat. If you like your meat cooked more than rare or medium rare, add about 3 minutes to the cooking time for each side, or throw the steaks in the oven at 400°F (200°C) and cook the meat for 6–7 minutes after cooking it on the grill.

5. Let the steaks rest for 8–10 minutes after they're done, and then serve them with a drizzle of extra virgin olive oil and the vegetables on the side.

Coscie di Rana Saltimbocca con Cavolini di Bruxelles

(FROGS' LEGS SALTIMBOCCA WITH BRUSSELS SPROUTS)

IN THE SUMMERTIME, WHEN I WAS GROWING UP, MY BROTHER AND I USED TO GO TO A MOUNTAIN LAKE, NEAR OUR HOUSE IN BOLOGNA, WHERE WE LIKED TO COLLECT TADPOLES IN A LITTLE CUP. WE LOVED TO SEE THE LITTLE ONES SWIM AROUND AND EVENTUALLY BECOME LITTLE FROGS. MY MOM USED TO MAKE THIS DISH WITH A LITTLE LEMON AND BUTTER WHEN WE WERE JUST KIDS.

PREP TIME: *30 minutes* | COOKING TIME: *25 minutes* | SERVES: *4*

12 frogs' legs (or chicken legs)

1 cup (125g) all-purpose flour, as needed, to coat the frogs' legs

8 tablespoons (110) butter

12 slices prosciutto crudo (¼ pound [100g])

1 whole ball of fresh mozzarella (8 ounces [225g])

12 sage leaves

Juice of ½ lemon

1 tablespoon (16g) capers

¼ cup (60ml) white wine

Salt and pepper

40 Brussels sprouts

4 tablespoons (60ml) extra virgin olive oil

1 medium white onion, sliced thin

½ pound (230g) diced pancetta

INSTRUCTIONS

1. To make the frogs' legs: First, take the frogs' legs and dip them in the flour.

2. In a nonstick pan, melt 4 tablespoons (60g) of the butter over medium to high heat, and sear the frogs' legs for about 3 minutes on each side to caramelize the surface and seal in the juices. Remove the frogs' legs from the pan and let them rest for a few minutes until they're cool enough to handle.

3. Preheat the oven to 400°F (200°C).

4. Wrap a slice of prosciutto, a piece of mozzarella, and a sage leaf around each of the 12 frogs' legs. Lay them on a sheet pan lined with parchment paper and bake them for 7 minutes. Take the frogs' legs out of the oven and let them rest.

5. To make the saltimbocca sauce: While the frogs' legs are resting, melt 4 tablespoons (60g) of the butter in a saucepan and add the lemon juice, capers, and the white wine. Cook this mixture until all the alcohol evaporates and then add a pinch of salt.

6. To make the Brussels sprouts: Rinse the Brussels sprouts under cold water and cut them in half. Fill a saucepan with water and boil the Brussels sprouts for about 8 minutes.

7. In another pan, heat the olive oil and add the onions. Cook the onions until they become translucent. Add the pancetta, and cook it until it becomes crispy, and then add the boiled Brussels sprouts and a pinch of salt and pepper. Continue to sauté the mixture for at least 10 minutes until it starts to become slightly crunchy.

8. Serve the frogs' legs on a bed of Brussels sprouts and topped with saltimbocca sauce.

Filetto di Maiale con Salsa al Latte

(PORK TENDERLOIN WITH MILK SAUCE)

THIS RECIPE MAKES A LOT OF EXTRA SAUCE, SO IT'S THE PERFECT DISH TO FARE *LA SCARPETTA*, WHICH MEANS TO MOP YOUR PLATE CLEAN WITH SOME GOOD BREAD!

PREP TIME: *10 minutes* | COOKING TIME: *30 minutes* | SERVES: *4*

INGREDIENTS

2 pounds (1kg) pork tenderloin

½ teaspoon cayenne pepper

Salt and pepper

8–12 tablespoons (60–100ml) extra virgin olive oil, divided

1–2 quarts (1–2L) whole milk

2 garlic cloves, crushed

1 red bell pepper, chopped

1 green bell pepper, chopped

1 yellow bell pepper, chopped

INSTRUCTIONS

1. Season the pork tenderloin with cayenne pepper, salt, and pepper. In a saucepan, heat 4–6 tablespoons (60–100ml) olive oil. Once the oil is hot, give the tenderloin a nice sear all over, about 7–8 minutes. This will seal in the juices.

2. Add the milk to the pan and cover it with a lid. Keep cooking the meat over medium to low heat, checking it every 10 minutes. Flip the meat periodically so it will absorb the flavor of the milk. Check the meat every 10 minutes and add more milk, as it cooks down, so there is always enough milk to cover the meat. Continue this process until the meat is fully cooked. Test for doneness with a meat thermometer. When the internal temperature reaches at least 145°F (60°C), remove the meat from the pan and let it rest.

3. Continue cooking the milk in the pan over medium to low heat, and add more milk, if needed, until you have a thick sauce.

4. In another pan, place 4–6 tablespoons (60–100 ml) olive oil, crushed garlic, bell peppers, and a pinch of the salt and pepper. Cook the mixture over medium heat for about 8 minutes.

5. Slice the pork and serve the bell peppers on the side. Pour the milk sauce over the pork and serve.

Branzino alla Erbe in Crosta di Sale

(SALT-ENCRUSTED SEA BASS)

BAKING FISH IN A SALT CRUST IS AN ANCIENT COOKING TECHNIQUE, AND ONE OF THE HEALTHIEST, TOO, BECAUSE THIS METHOD DOESN'T REQUIRE ANY ADDED OIL OR BUTTER. INSTEAD, THE FISH COOKS IN ITS OWN FAT, INSIDE A COATING OF SALT AND EGG WHITES. SOME PEOPLE USE WATER INSTEAD OF EGG WHITES IN THE SALT MIXTURE, BUT THAT SHOULD NOT BE DONE, BECAUSE THE WATER EVAPORATES DURING COOKING AND BREAKS THE SALT BARRIER. THE RESULT: DRY FISH. TO AVOID THIS, BE SURE TO USE EGG WHITES IN MAKING THE SALT CRUST.

PREP TIME: *30 minutes* | COOKING TIME: *30 minutes* | SERVES: *2*

FOR THE FISH

1 whole, 1¾-pounds (800g) sea bass

6 sprigs thyme, chopped fine

5–6 sage leaves, chopped

1 tablespoon (5g) fresh parsley, chopped

3 rosemary sprigs, chopped

Zest of 1 lemon

1 clove garlic, minced

6–8 tablespoons (100–120ml) extra virgin olive oil, plus more for drizzling

Juice of 1 lemon

FOR THE SALT CRUST

3–4 egg whites

4 cups (800g) table salt

5 cups (1kg) kosher salt

INSTRUCTIONS

1. To prepare the sea bass: Using the dull side of a knife, held at a 45-degree angle with the sharp side facing toward you, scrape away from yourself to remove all the scales from the fish. To gut the fish, use a paring knife to cut open the belly, starting near the tail and cutting up to the base of the gills. Spread the abdominal cavity with your fingers, remove all the entrails, and rinse out the cavity as thoroughly as possible. Dry the fish with paper towels. To save time, you can ask your fishmonger to do the job.

2. After the fish has been gutted and cleaned, combine the herbs, lemon zest, garlic, and 6–8 tablespoons (100–120ml) olive oil in a small bowl and mix them together. Reserve 2 tablespoons (30g) of the herb mixture for the salt/egg white crust. Stuff the rest of the herb mixture inside the fish.

3. To make the salt crust: In a stand mixer with a whisk attachment or a handheld mixer with whisk, whip the egg whites until they form stiff peaks (about 5 minutes). Gently incorporate the reserved 2 tablespoons (30g) of the herb mixture into the egg whites. Next, add the table salt and kosher salt to the egg white mixture. It should be dense but spreadable. If the mixture becomes too dense, whip an extra egg white and add it to the mix.

4. Place a piece of parchment paper on a rimmed baking sheet or jelly roll pan so that it covers the bottom of the pan but does not drape over the sides. Spread a layer of the whipped salt/egg white mixture on the parchment paper. Lay the fish on top and completely cover the fish with the remaining salt/egg white mixture.

5. To make the fish: Preheat the oven to 350°F (180°C).

6. Bake the fish for 30 minutes. When you take the fish out of the oven, the salt mixture should be hard and the fish should be completely encrusted in the mixture. With a hammer, crack open the salt crust and remove the fish. It should be perfectly seasoned. Be careful not to get any salt on the fish when removing it from the crust.

7. Squeeze some lemon juice over the fish and add a splash of olive oil to enhance the flavor.

Filetto di Branzino con Teste di Asparagi e Purée di Cavolfiore

(SEA BASS FILET WITH ASPARAGUS TIPS AND CAULIFLOWER PURÉE)

WHEN I WAS GROWING UP IN LUCCA, TUSCANY, MY PARENTS RENTED A HOUSE ON THE BEACH AT VIAREGGIO FOR THE WHOLE SUMMER. MY GRANDMA AND GREAT-AUNT TOOK CARE OF THE WHOLE FAMILY WHEN THEY VISITED US. ONE OF MY GRANDMA'S BEST DISHES WAS PAN-FRIED SEA BASS, WHICH SHE USUALLY SERVED WITH FRIED POTATOES—A SIDE DISH I LOVED. AS I GREW OLDER, I DEVELOPED A TASTE FOR MANY OTHERS, INCLUDING THIS AMAZING CAULIFLOWER DISH. THE CREAMINESS AND DELICATE FLAVOR OF THE CAULIFLOWER PERFECTLY COMPLEMENT THE FISH.

PREP TIME: *10 minutes* | COOKING TIME: *35 minutes* | SERVES: *4*

1 pint (475ml) milk

1 pint (475ml) heavy cream

Salt and pepper to taste

6 tablespoons (90ml) extra virgin olive oil

Head of 1 medium-size cauliflower, broken into florets

1 golden potato, diced

6 tablespoons (85g) butter

½ cup (40g) parmigiano, grated

1 teaspoon (2.5g) nutmeg

8 cloves garlic, 1 clove for each filet

8 sprigs thyme, 1 sprig for each filet

Eight 4–6 ounce (113–170g) sea bass filets

30–32 asparagus tips

Juice of 1 lemon (optional)

INSTRUCTIONS

1. To make the cauliflower purée: Pour the milk and cream into a saucepan with a pinch of salt and the olive oil, and bring the mixture to a boil. Add the cauliflower, potato, and butter and cook gently over low to medium heat for 15–20 minutes.

2. When the vegetables are cooked and have softened, add the grated parmigiano and the nutmeg. Use an immersion blender to thoroughly blend the mixture while it is still hot.

3. To make the fish, one filet at a time: Heat some olive oil in a nonstick pan and add 1 clove of garlic and 1 sprig of thyme. Once the pan gets very hot, add 1 of the 8 sea bass filets. If the pan is not hot enough, the fish will stick to it and break apart. Season the filet with a little salt and pepper and cook it for about 2–3 minutes on each side.

4. Remove the fish from the pan. (Sometimes all of the fish fillets won't fit in the oven at the same time, so it is a good idea to place the pan in the oven and cook 4 at the time if they don't fit.) After all the fish are cooked, place the asparagus tips in the same pan used for the fish and cook them over medium heat for about 5 minutes.

5. Serve each sea bass filet on top of the cauliflower purée and garnish the fish with the asparagus tips. Squeeze a bit of lemon juice on the fish, if you like, and enjoy it hot.

Pesce Spada con Insalata e Noci Pecan

(SWORDFISH WITH BUTTER LETTUCE AND PECANS)

IN THE SUMMERTIME, I USED TO GO FISHING WITH MY UNCLE VINCENZO IN VIAREGGIO. AFTERWARD WE WOULD GO TO A LOCAL RESTAURANT THAT SERVED FANTASTIC SWORDFISH THAT WOULD JUST MELT IN YOUR MOUTH—PERFECT WITH A NICE, CRISP SALAD.

PREP TIME: *15 minutes* | COOKING TIME: *15 minutes* | SERVES: *4*

FOR THE FISH

3 cloves garlic, finely chopped

½ bunch fresh Italian parsley, chopped

Pinch of crushed red pepper

Juice of 1 lemon

4 tablespoons (60ml) extra virgin olive oil

Four 4–6 ounce (113–170g) swordfish filets

Salt and pepper to taste

FOR THE SALAD

1 small head butter lettuce

½ cup (65g) pecans, chopped

½ cup (80g) cherry tomatoes, quartered

1 tablespoon (15ml) balsamic vinegar

INSTRUCTIONS

1. To make the swordfish: In a large bowl, mix together the garlic, parsley, crushed red pepper, lemon juice, and 1 tablespoon (15ml) of the olive oil. Marinate the swordfish by massaging it with the olive oil mixture, and then let the fish rest in the marinade for 15 minutes.

2. While the swordfish is marinating, heat the grill to high. Once the swordfish is done marinating, grill the fish over high heat for 5–7 minutes on each side. Add salt and pepper to taste.

3. To make the salad: Chop up the butter lettuce and put it in a bowl. Add the pecans and cherry tomatoes and toss them, with the lettuce, in the remaining olive oil, the balsamic vinegar, and salt and pepper to taste.

4. Plate the salad next to the swordfish and enjoy it with a nice glass of white wine from Italy!

Pollo alla Milanese con Porcini Fritti e Rucola

(CHICKEN MILANESE WITH FRIED PORCINI MUSHROOMS AND ARUGULA SALAD)

EATING FRIED PORCINI MUSHROOMS HAS BEEN A TRADITION IN MY HOME SINCE I WAS A KID. USUALLY, YOU CAN FIND PORCINI EARLY IN SEPTEMBER, IF IT'S BEEN WET, SINCE RAIN IS THE KEY TO THEIR GROWTH. IF IT'S BEEN A DRY SUMMER, YOU WON'T FIND THEM AROUND. I HAVE MEMORIES OF MY DAD AND MOM IN THE KITCHEN, MAKING PORCINI WITH CHICKEN (OR TRYING TO!), AND MY DAD GETTING MAD AT ME FOR EATING ALL THE MUSHROOMS BEFORE THEY COULD GET INTO THE DISH—AND LEAVING NONE FOR ANYONE ELSE.

PREP TIME: *70 minutes* | COOKING TIME: *15 minutes* | SERVES: *4*

4 eggs

6 boneless chicken breasts

2 cups (470ml) sunflower oil for frying

Enough all-purpose flour to coat the chicken

Enough bread crumbs to coat the chicken

3 ounces (85g) arugula

4 tablespoons (60ml) extra virgin olive oil

1 lemon

Salt and pepper to taste

12 cherry tomatoes, half cut

Parmigiano, shaved, for garnish

½ pound (230g) porcini mushrooms

Enough cornmeal to coat the porcini mushrooms (approximately 1 cup [120g])

INSTRUCTIONS

1. To make the chicken: In a large bowl, whisk the eggs and let the chicken breasts sit in the beaten eggs. Cover the bowl with plastic wrap and put it in the fridge for about 1 hour. A few minutes before removing the chicken from the fridge, heat the sunflower oil in a large frying pan and bring it to 350°F (180°C). (Use a probe thermometer to check the temperature of the oil.)

2. Take the chicken breasts out of the fridge and coat them, first in the flour, and then in the bread crumbs. Fry the chicken breasts for about 3–4 minutes on each side or until they've turned golden brown. Transfer the chicken breasts to a plate lined with paper towels to absorb any excess oil.

3. To make the salad: Dress the arugula with the olive oil, a squeeze of the lemon, and salt and pepper to taste. Add the cherry tomatoes and parmigiano.

4. To make the porcini mushrooms: Thinly slice the porcini mushrooms. Coat them in some of the cornmeal and deep-fry them in the same oil as you used for the chicken for 4–5 minutes or until they're crispy.

5. Place the chicken on the salad, with the porcini mushrooms on top.

Pollo Burro e Salvia con Patate Arrostite in Padella

(BROWN BUTTER SAGE CHICKEN WITH FINGERLING POTATOES)

THIS IS THE SIMPLEST, QUICKEST DINNER TO MAKE WHEN YOU COME HOME LATE FROM WORK. IT'S ONE OF MY FAMILY'S FAVORITES.

PREP TIME: *10 minutes* | COOKING TIME: *30 minutes* | SERVES: *4*

FOR THE CHICKEN

2 cups (250g) flour, or more, for coating

Four 4-ounce (120g) chicken breasts, pounded thin (to about half of the original thickness)

8 tablespoons (110g) butter

16 fresh sage leaves

Salt and pepper to taste

2 tablespoons (30g) butter (optional)

FOR THE POTATOES

2 pounds (1kg) fingerling potatoes

2 tablespoons (30g) olive oil

2 cloves garlic, crushed

1 sprig rosemary, chopped

Salt and pepper to taste

INSTRUCTIONS

1. To make the chicken: Pour the flour onto a large plate. Dredge the chicken breasts in the flour to coat them completely. Place the flour-coated chicken breasts on another plate and set it aside.

2. Place 8 tablespoons (110g) of butter in a medium saucepan. When the butter begins to melt, add the sage. Cook the mixture until the butter turns slightly brown and the sage is crispy. Add the chicken breasts to the pan with a generous shake of salt and pepper and cook them over medium heat on each side until they're golden brown. Cook the chicken for about 3 minutes on each. Transfer the chicken from the pan to a warm plate. If you'd like a little sauce for the chicken, add 2 tablespoons (30g) of butter to the pan with the remaining sage and cook it until it turns golden. Pour the sauce over your chicken.

3. To make the potatoes: Boil the potatoes for approximately 8 minutes in boiling salted water until they're soft. Remove the potatoes from the boiling water and let them cool slightly. When they're cool enough to handle, cut the potatoes into quarters.

4. Place the olive oil and crushed garlic in a large saucepan. Add the potatoes and rosemary to the pan and cook the potatoes on medium to high heat for about 6–7minutes, until they turn golden brown.

My Father's Roast Beef

MY FATHER'S ROAST BEEF IS FAST AND VERY TASTY. ALL IT NEEDS IS SOME SALT AND PEPPER AND, SURPRISINGLY, A MICROWAVE.

PREP TIME: *5 minutes* | COOKING TIME: *10 minutes* | SERVES: *6–8*

1 pound (500g) roast beef

Pepper to taste, enough to cover
the meat

6 tablespoons (100ml) extra virgin
olive oil

Salt to taste

INSTRUCTIONS

1. Coat the roast beef with pepper, put it in a microwavable bowl, and then cover the microwavable bowl with another such bowl. Microwave the roast beef for 3–4 minutes. Flip the roast beef and cook it on the other side, uncovered, for an additional 3–4 minutes. Then sprinkle the meat with a little salt, to taste, and the olive oil. Cover the meat and let it rest for 10 minutes before serving. Then put it on a cutting board and slice it thin with a meat knife.

ZUPPE

(SOUPS)

WHETHER IT'S A HARDY LENTIL SOUP OR A VELVETY BOWL OF CREAM OF MUSHROOM YOU CRAVE, YOU'LL FIND SOME GREAT OPTIONS TO SATISFY YOUR TASTE BUDS—AND YOUR SOUL—IN THIS CHAPTER. THE GOODNESS OF A BOWL OF SOUP IS UNQUESTIONED ALL OVER ITALY, FROM NORTH TO SOUTH, AND THE TRADITION OF MAKING IT VARIES, ALWAYS WITH DELICIOUS RESULTS, FROM PLACE TO PLACE. WHEN I WAS GROWING UP, MY DAD WAS THE SOUP COOK. JUST THINKING ABOUT THE SOUPS HE MADE BRINGS BACK AMAZING MEMORIES.

PASTA E FAGIOLI   80

(Pasta and Bean Soup)

VELLUTATA DI FUNGHI   82

(Cream of Mushroom Soup)

RIBOLLITA TOSCANA   84

(Tuscan Bread Soup)

FARINATA LUCCHESE   87

(Cornmeal Soup from Lucca)

ZUPPA DI LENTICCHIE   89

(Lentil Soup)

CREMA DI ASPARAGI   90

(Cream of Asparagus Soup)

Pasta e Fagioli

(PASTA AND BEAN SOUP)

THIS RECIPE FOR PASTA AND BEAN SOUP HAS BEEN IN MY FAMILY FOR GENERATIONS. MY DAD STILL MAKES IT, AND HAS TAUGHT ME HOW TO PREPARE IT, TOO. IN THE ITALIAN COUNTRYSIDE, BEANS ARE OFTEN USED IN PLACE OF PASTA, PARTICULARLY THE TAGLIERINI MADE BY THE POPULAR BRAND, AVE MARIA.

PREP TIME: *24 hours, 15 minutes* | COOKING TIME: *1 hour 40 minutes* | SERVES: *4*

INGREDIENTS

- 2 cups (400g) dried beans, such as pinto or cannellini

- 2 sprigs sage

- 6 cloves garlic

- 3–4 tablespoons (45–100ml) extra virgin olive oil

- 1 small onion

- 1 carrot

- 1 celery stalk, chopped

- 2 sprigs rosemary

- 6–8 fresh marjoram leaves

- 7 ounces (200g) pancetta, chopped

- 1 tablespoon (16g) tomato paste

- Salt and black pepper to taste

- 1¼ cups (250g) pasta, such as elbow, ditalini, or any dried flat pasta, like lasagna, broken into small pieces

INSTRUCTIONS

1. Place the beans in a large bowl or stockpot. Cover them with water and let them soak overnight at room temperature.

2. Drain the beans. Fill a large stockpot with water, add 1 sprig of sage and 2 cloves of garlic, and bring it to a boil. Add the beans and let them simmer for about 1 hour.

3. Meanwhile, in a medium saucepan, heat the olive oil over medium heat. Chop the vegetables and the remaining garlic into small pieces and add them to the pan, along with 1 sprig of sage, the rosemary (just the leaves), and marjoram. Sauté the mixture until it begins to turn golden brown. Add the pancetta and let it brown. Then add the tomato paste and dilute it with a cup of water from the pot of beans that are still cooking on the stove. Let the mixture thicken 5 minutes or so and turn off the heat.

4. When the beans are almost done, but still cooking, add a little salt. When they're done, transfer the beans, and the water from the stockpot, along with the seasonings from the saucepan, to a blender or food processor and purée. Season the mixture with a little salt and black pepper. Put the puréed bean mix back into the stockpot on the stove over medium heat. When it starts to boil, add the pasta and cook for 2–3 minutes if using fresh pasta and 8–11 minutes if using dry pasta. Divide the pasta and beans into bowls and serve immediately with some crusty bread.

Vellutata di Funghi

(CREAM OF MUSHROOM SOUP)

DURING THE WINTER, THERE IS NOTHING BETTER THAN A BOWL OF WARM AND CREAMY MUSHROOM SOUP. IN ITALY, IT SNOWS IN THE WINTERTIME, AND GETS REALLY COLD, SO MY GRANDMA WOULD ALWAYS WARM US UP WITH A SOUP MADE WITH THE MUSHROOMS THAT MY GRANDPA FOUND IN THE FOREST NEARBY.

PREP TIME: *15 minutes* | COOKING TIME: *40 minutes* | SERVES: *4*

INGREDIENTS

4 tablespoons (60ml) extra virgin olive oil

1 large (3 ounces [80g]) leek, chopped

20 ounces (100g) button mushrooms, plus a few extra for garnish, sliced approximately ¼ inch (6mm) thick

2 medium-size potatoes (10 ounces [300g]) sliced or diced

Salt and pepper to taste

3 cups (700 ml) milk

INSTRUCTIONS

1. In a large, nonstick stockpot, heat 3 tablespoons (45g) of the olive oil, and then add the chopped leek. Cook it until it is golden and translucent. Add the mushrooms and cook them with the chopped leek for another 5–7 minutes over medium heat. Now add the potatoes and a pinch or two of salt and pepper, and continue to stir and sauté the mixture for another 5 minutes. Finally, add the milk and cover the pot with a lid. Cook the mixture for another 20 minutes over medium to low heat and then remove the lid and cook for 5 more minutes.

2. Remove the stockpot from the heat while the mixture is still hot, and use an immersion blender to blend it well. Then strain the mixture through a cheesecloth or chinois (a conical sieve with an extremely fine mesh).

3. Finally, julienne the mushrooms you set aside for the garnish. Add the last tablespoon of olive oil to a small saucepan and sauté the mushrooms, with a little salt and pepper, until they're crispy. Top the soup with the crispy mushrooms and enjoy it hot or warm.

Ribollita Toscana

(TUSCAN BREAD SOUP)

RIBOLLITA IS A PERFECT EXAMPLE OF TUSCAN CUISINE. IT CAME INTO BEING
WHEN FARMERS HAD NO MONEY TO BUY FOOD AND COULD ONLY USE THEIR OWN
VEGETABLES TO FEED THEIR FAMILIES—TO MAKE SURE THEY HAD ENOUGH ENERGY
TO CONTINUE WORKING IN THE FIELDS. DURING THE WINTERTIME, MY MOM LOVES
TO MAKE ALL SORTS OF SOUPS WITH MIXED VEGETABLES AND OLD BREAD. AS IT
HAPPENS, INGREDIENTS LIKE VEGETABLES AND BREAD ARE ALWAYS ON THE TABLE
OF EVERY GOOD ITALIAN, AND, AS A CULTURE, IT IS TRADITIONAL FOR US TO HAVE
BREAD WITH EVERY MEAL!

PREP TIME: *24 hours, 15 minutes* | COOKING TIME: *approximately 40 minutes* | SERVES: *4*

INGREDIENTS

Four 15-ounce (400g) cans cannellini beans

2 tablespoons (30g) salt, plus salt and pepper to taste

7 tablespoons (105ml) extra virgin olive oil, plus more for serving

4 sprigs fresh thyme

2 carrots, chopped

1 onion, chopped

2 garlic cloves, minced

2 celery stalks, chopped

2 medium-size potatoes, thinly sliced

1 tablespoon (15ml) tomato paste

35 leaves Tuscan kale, chopped

½ Savoy cabbage, chopped

28 Swiss chard leaves, chopped

2 loaves stale bread, such as ciabatta or rustic baguettes, sliced

INSTRUCTIONS

1. Put the beans in a large bowl or stockpot. Cover them with water and let them soak overnight at room temperature.

2. Drain the beans and fill a large stockpot with water. Put the beans in the large stockpot and fill it with 2 quarts (2L) of water and 2 tablespoons (30g) of salt. Cook the beans for 1 hour.

3. When they are cooked, remove ¾ of the beans from the stockpot, without discarding the water, and set them aside. Blend the water and the remaining beans in the stockpot with an immersion blender. Then put the reserved beans back into the stockpot.

4. In a pan over medium to high heat, heat 5 tablespoons (75ml) of the olive oil and add the fresh thyme, carrots, onion, garlic, and celery and cook them for about 6–8 minutes, until they turn golden. Then add the potatoes and the tomato paste with 1 cup (240 ml) of water to the pan and let the mixture simmer for a few more minutes. Add salt to taste, along with the kale, cabbage, and Swiss chard. Let them wilt in the pan. Add the beans and let them simmer for another hour on low heat, adding a little water, if the mixture becomes too thick.

5. Now add the sliced bread to the soup and give it a stir. Let it cook for a few more minutes over medium to low heat. Take it off the heat and let the soup rest as long as possible, preferably overnight, for the best result. Ribollita means "reboiled," so the day after you've made the soup, bring it to a boil for a few minutes and serve it with a touch of extra virgin olive oil and some freshly cracked pepper.

Farinata Lucchese

FARINATA IS A VARIATION OF RIBOLLITA, A CLASSIC DISH FROM MY HOMETOWN OF LUCCA, AND, OF COURSE, IT HAS BEEN A STAPLE OF FARMING VILLAGES FOR CENTURIES. IN THIS VARIATION OF RIBOLLITA, CORNMEAL IS USED INSTEAD OF BREAD, AND THE SOUP IS NOT "REBOILED."

PREP TIME: *2½ hours* | COOKING TIME: *2 hours* | SERVES: *4*

INGREDIENTS

1 pound (500g) red beans

2 sprigs sage

4 garlic cloves

Salt and pepper to taste

½ cup (120ml) extra virgin olive oil, plus more for drizzling

2 carrots, chopped

2 stalks celery, chopped

1 onion, diced

3½ ounces (100g) pancetta, cubed

1 teaspoon (5g) tomato paste

2 potatoes, chopped

1 leek, chopped

14 ounces (400g) Savoy cabbage, chopped

10 ounces (300g) Tuscan kale, chopped

2 cups (300g) cornmeal

INSTRUCTIONS

1. Put the beans in a large stockpot. Cover them with water and let them soak overnight at room temperature.

2. Drain the beans and put them back in the stockpot with 2–3 quarts (2–3L) of fresh water. Add 1 of the sage sprigs and 2 garlic cloves to the pot and bring the water to a boil.

3. When the beans are almost done, add a little salt to taste.

4. In a large stockpot, heat all of the olive oil and sauté 2 of the garlic gloves, the rest of the sage, and the carrots, celery, and onion for about 5 minutes or until soft. Add the pancetta and sauté for about 2–3 minutes until everything is golden and the pancetta is cooked. Add the tomato paste with a cup of the water from the cooked beans.

5. Now add the potatoes, leek, cabbage, and kale to the stockpot and cook for a few minutes until the cabbage and kale leaves have wilted, then add half the cooked beans. Blend the other half of the beans with an immersion blender or in a food processor, and add them to the stockpot. Mix everything well and add more hot water from the cooked beans, and salt and pepper as needed. Cover the stockpot with a lid and let the soup simmer for at least 1½ hours over low heat. Simmering will release the flavor from all the ingredients in this incredible soup.

6. After 1½ hours or so, add the cornmeal, quickly stirring it with a whisk to prevent any lumps from forming. Continue to cook the soup for another 35 minutes or more, stirring it every couple of minutes with a big wooden spoon. Once the soup is cooked, serve it immediately with a drizzle of extra virgin olive oil on top.

Farinata Fritta

(LEFTOVER FRIED FARINATA SOUP)

THIS IS A GREAT RIFF ON *FARINATA LUCCHESE* (SEE PAGE 87) AND AN EASY WAY TO USE THE LEFTOVERS TO MAKE A DELICIOUS SIDE DISH OR SNACK.

INSTRUCTIONS

1. Simply refrigerate the *Farinata Lucchese* soup overnight. As it cools, the soup will solidify, thanks to the cornmeal.

2. Cut the solidified soup into 1-inch (3cm) thick portions. Pour a drizzle of extra virgin olive oil onto a hot pan and fry each side for 3–4 minutes over low to medium heat.

Zuppa di Lenticchie

(LENTIL SOUP)

IN ITALY, IT IS TRADITIONAL TO ENJOY LENTIL SOUP AROUND CHRISTMAS AND THE NEW YEAR, WHEN THE SOUP IS EATEN WITH *COTECHINO*, A LARGE PORK SAUSAGE. ADDING THIS SAUSAGE TO THE SOUP IS A DELICIOUS WAY TO USE UP ANY LEFTOVER *COTECHINO*.

PREP TIME: *24 hours, 10 minutes* | COOKING TIME: *2 hours, 10 minutes* | SERVES: *4*

1 cup (200g) lentils

3 tablespoons (45ml) extra virgin olive oil

2 garlic cloves, minced

2 carrots, chopped

2 celery stalks, chopped

2 small potatoes, diced

1 onion, chopped

2 small zucchini, diced

1 teaspoon cumin

2½ quarts (2.5L) water

2 bay leaves

Salt and pepper to taste

INSTRUCTIONS

1. Soak the lentils overnight or for at least 12 hours.

2. In a medium stockpot, heat all the olive oil and sauté the garlic and all the vegetables until they are golden and translucent. Add the lentils, cumin, water, and bay leaves.

3. Cover the pot and simmer the soup over low heat for about 2 hours. Add salt and pepper to taste. Remove the bay leaves before serving the soup and enjoy it with a nice loaf of crusty bread.

Crema di Asparagi

(CREAM OF ASPARAGUS SOUP)

CREAM OF ASPARAGUS SOUP IS A CLASSIC, LIGHT, AND DELICATE SPRING DISH, WITH A LOT OF FLAVOR. MY MOM PREPARED IT MANY TIMES FROM THE FRESH ASPARAGUS WE PICKED FROM OUR OWN GARDEN, WHEN IT WAS IN SEASON. THE ASPARAGUS WAS ALSO DELICIOUS PREPARED IN RISOTTO OR SIMPLY BOILED AND SERVED WITH A DRIZZLE OF GOOD-QUALITY OLIVE OIL.

PREP TIME: *10 minutes* | COOKING TIME: *45 minutes* | SERVES: *4*

INGREDIENTS

1 bunch (2 pounds [1kg]) asparagus

3 tablespoons (45ml) extra virgin olive oil

2 tablespoons (30g) butter

1 or 2 shallots, depending on size, sliced

2 medium-size yellow potatoes, such as Yukon Gold, diced

½ cup (120ml) white wine

Salt and white pepper to taste

1 quart (1L) vegetable broth

1 cup (240ml) heavy cream

1 garlic clove, crushed

INSTRUCTIONS

1. Chop the asparagus, except for the tips. Set the asparagus tips aside.

2. In a large nonstick pan, heat 1 tablespoon (15ml) of the olive oil and melt the butter. Cook the shallots for 2–3 minutes in the pan. Add the potatoes and chopped asparagus and cook the mixture for 8 more minutes, stirring it to make sure the vegetables don't stick to the bottom of the pan.

3. After the asparagus and potatoes are done (they will be soft), transfer them to a bowl while you deglaze the pan with some of the white wine. Let it cook off over medium to low heat. Add salt and pepper to taste. Put the potatoes and asparagus back into the pan and add the vegetable broth. Cook the mixture for another 20 minutes or until the vegetables have softened.

4. Add the heavy cream and cook the soup for 10 more minutes. Take it off the heat and, using an immersion blender, purée the mixture while it is still hot (use caution when blending hot liquids). Strain the soup through a cheesecloth or chinois (a conical sieve with an extremely fine mesh) to remove any unwanted fibers from the asparagus.

5. In a small saucepan, heat 2 tablespoons (30ml) of the olive oil and sauté the asparagus tips with the garlic. Cook the asparagus tips over medium heat until they're slightly crunchy and caramelized. Serve the soup in a large bowl garnished with the crispy asparagus tips on top.

INSALATE FREDDE

(COLD SALADS)

COLD SALADS ARE A REAL LIFELINE DURING THE SUMMER, WHEN THE TEMPERATURE RISES AND THERE IS LITTLE DESIRE TO DO MUCH COOKING OVER A HOT STOVE.

Insalata di Farro con Gamberi

(FARRO SALAD WITH SHRIMP)

FARRO IS A KIND OF WHEAT THAT WAS FIRST CULTIVATED ABOUT TEN THOUSAND YEARS AGO. HISTORICALLY, IT HAS BEEN USED IN SALADS AND SOUPS IN GARFAGNANA, IN THE MOUNTAINS OF LUCCA, AS LONG AS WE CAN REMEMBER. THE FARRO, SHRIMP, AND FRESH VEGGIES IN THIS RECIPE MAKE A COMPLETE, ENERGIZING, ONE-DISH MEAL, PERFECT FOR THE SUMMERTIME. YOU CAN SERVE IT COLD OR AT ROOM TEMPERATURE. IT USUALLY TASTES BETTER THE NEXT DAY, AFTER THE FARRO HAS ABSORBED ALL THE FLAVORS OF THE OTHER INGREDIENTS IN THE SALAD.

PREP TIME: *20 minutes* | COOKING TIME: *30 minutes* | SERVES: *4*

INGREDIENTS

1½ cups (240g) farro

5 tablespoons (75ml) extra virgin olive oil, to dress the salad

4 cloves garlic, minced

¾ cup (350g) cherry tomatoes, sliced

½ cup (75g) green olives, chopped

2 zucchini, diced

1 red bell pepper, chopped

1 red chili pepper, sliced julienne

24 shrimp, shelled and deveined

Salt and pepper to taste

16 basil leaves, chopped

INSTRUCTIONS

1. In a large stockpot, cook the farro in boiling water for about 20 minutes. When the farro is done (when it is soft like rice) drain and transfer it to a bowl, and let it cool in the fridge for about 20–25 minutes.

2. Add 2 tablespoons (30ml) olive oil, the minced garlic, cherry tomatoes, and olives to the cool farro.

3. In a medium saucepan, heat 3 tablespoons (45ml) of olive oil and sauté the zucchini, bell pepper, and chili pepper over medium to high heat for about 5 minutes. Once the zucchini and peppers start to get soft, add the shrimp and a dash of salt and pepper. Cook for about 3 minutes. Once the shrimp finish cooking (they will be pink and there will be caramelization around them), add the shrimp and veggie mixture to the farro and mix in the chopped basil. Serve the salad cold or at room temperature.

Insalata di Salmone

(SALMON SALAD)

AT CARRARA PASTRIES, THIS SALMON SALAD IS THE MOST POPULAR ITEM ON THE MENU. I SELL MORE THAN 50 POUNDS (25KG) OF IT EVERY WEEK!

PREP TIME: *10 minutes* | COOKING TIME: *10 minutes* | SERVES: *4*

INGREDIENTS

3 ounces (85g) mixed baby greens

1 mango, pitted and diced

1 tomato, pitted and sliced

1 carrot, shaved

1 avocado, cubed

Salt and pepper to taste

Extra virgin olive oil and balsamic vinegar to dress the salad, plus more for drizzling

1 cucumber, sliced thin

Four 6-ounce (170g) salmon steaks

1 lemon, quartered

INSTRUCTIONS

1. In a mixing bowl, combine the baby greens, mango, tomato, carrot, and avocado with some salt and pepper, and drizzle with some olive oil and a dash of balsamic vinegar. Toss everything together. Plate the salad and garnish with the cucumber slices.

2. Season the salmon with salt and pepper and a drizzle of olive oil. Preheat a grill on high and cook the salmon for 2 minutes on each side. Take the salmon off the grill and cook it for 5–7 minutes in a preheated oven at 350°F (180°C).

3. Serve the salmon with the salad on the side and a squeeze of lemon. Enjoy!

Insalata di Pasta Fredda

(COLD PASTA SALAD)

WHEN SUMMER HAS ARRIVED, AND YOU DON'T WANT TO EAT ANYTHING HOT, THIS IS THE PERFECT DISH TO BRING TO WORK OR A PICNIC—IT'S SO COOL AND REFRESHING.

PREP TIME: *20 minutes* | COOKING TIME: *25 minutes* | SERVES: *4*

1 zucchini, cut long like julienne

1 carrot

1½ cups (200g) cherry tomatoes

2 tablespoons (30ml) extra virgin olive oil

1½ cups (200g) peas

4 cups (250g) fusilli pasta

Salt and pepper to taste

3½ ounces (100g) mortadella, sliced

3½ ounces (100g) Swiss cheese, cubed

1 teaspoon (3g) thyme leaves, to sprinkle on top

10 basil leaves

INSTRUCTIONS

1. Julienne the zucchini and the carrot, and slice the cherry tomatoes. Cook the zucchini and carrots in pan with 2 tablespoons (30ml) of olive oil and a pinch of salt for 3 minutes on high heat. Cook the peas in water for at least 10–12 minutes on medium heat, with a pinch of salt.

2. In a large pot, boil some water and cook the fusilli for about 5–6 minutes. Immediately cool the pasta in an ice bath to halt the cooking process and keep the pasta from overcooking. You want it to be al dente. Strain the pasta, making sure to get rid of as much water as possible. If the pasta is too wet, it will not mix well with the olive oil or taste good, either, so make sure it is as dry as possible.

3. Once you have removed all the excess water from the pasta, transfer it to a large bowl and mix in the olive oil and veggies. Add the sliced mortadella and Swiss cheese. Garnish the salad with the thyme and basil leaves, and serve it cold or at room temperature.

Insalata con Tagliata di Manzo

(STEAK SALAD)

TAGLIATA DI MANZO SIMPLY REFERS TO A METHOD OF SLICING STEAK AGAINST THE GRAIN IN THIN STRIPS. TRADITIONALLY, THE STEAK IS GRILLED FIRST AND THEN SLICED AND SERVED WITH ARUGULA AND SHAVED PARMIGIANO.

PREP TIME: *20 minutes* | COOKING TIME: *25 minutes* | SERVES: *4*

INGREDIENTS

- 3–4 leaves radicchio, chopped
- 1 small head red leaf lettuce
- ¼ cup (15g) sun-dried tomatoes
- ¼ cup (30g) pine nuts
- 6–7 tablespoons (100–115ml) extra virgin olive oil
- Salt and pepper to taste
- 1 onion, sliced
- 1½ cups (55g) wild mushrooms, sliced
- 1 cup (240ml) white wine
- 2 cloves garlic
- 1 sprig rosemary
- 1 sprig sage
- 8–10-ounce (230–300g) skirt steak

INSTRUCTIONS

1. In a salad bowl, place the chopped radicchio and red leaf lettuce. Add the sun-dried tomatoes, pine nuts, 2–3 tablespoons (30–45ml) olive oil, and some salt and pepper. Toss to combine all the salad ingredients.

2. In a medium saucepan, heat 2 tablespoons (30ml) oil and add the sliced onion and mushrooms. Sauté them for at least 7 minutes, then add the wine and cook until all the wine evaporates. Set aside the onion and mushroom mixture and let it cool to room temperature. Once it has cooled, add it to the salad and toss everything together.

3. While the onions and mushrooms are cooling, start preparing the steak. First, finely chop the garlic and herbs and place them in a small mixing bowl with

2 tablespoons (30ml) of olive oil. Mix it well. Massage the steak with the herb mixture. Add a little salt and pepper to the meat and let it marinate for 15 minutes at room temperature.

4. While the steak is marinating, preheat your grill on high. Once it is nice and hot, sear the meat for 5 minutes on each side.

5. Remove the meat from the grill and finish cooking it in the oven at 400°F (200°C) for 6–7 more minutes.

6. Take the steak out of the oven and let it rest for 6–7 minutes. With a sharp chef's knife, slice the meat against the grain in strips, tagliata style. Serve it on a plate with the salad.

Insalata di Mare

(SEAFOOD SALAD)

THIS SEAFOOD SALAD IS PERFECT AS A LIGHT SUMMERTIME MEAL.

PREP TIME: *30 minutes* | COOKING TIME: *60 minutes* | SERVES: *4*

INGREDIENTS

1 pound (500g) shrimp

2 pounds (1kg) clams

2 pounds (1kg) mussels

1 pound (500g) squid

½ pound (500g) octopus

2 carrots, chopped

2 celery stalks, chopped

3 tablespoons (45ml) extra virgin olive oil

1 head garlic

1 tablespoon (5g) parsley, finely chopped

Salt and pepper to taste

¼ cup (60ml) lemon juice

INSTRUCTIONS

1. Start by cleaning all the fresh seafood or ask your fishmonger to do it for you. Remove the head and shell and devein all the shrimp. Rinse them under cold water and set them aside. Rinse the clams and mussels, cleaning the outer shell with a small brush to remove any dirt or sand. Remove the tongue that sticks out from the side of the mussels and rinse them again under cold water. Set them aside.

2. To clean the squid, slice it in half, just below the eyes, and separate the tentacles from the head. Reserve the tentacles. Then, holding the body, pull out the head, all the innards, and the skeleton. Discard them. Working from the cut end of the squid, peel back the skin toward the tip and discard it. Rinse out the inside of the squid and clean the tentacles with cold water. Slice the body of the squid crosswise into strips or rings and rinse them under cold water. Set them aside.

3. Clean the octopus by rinsing it well under cold water, tentacle by tentacle. Then remove the innards and the eyes and beak with a small sharp knife, and clean the inside of the head thoroughly with cold water. Use a meat tenderizer to tenderize the octopus, then rinse it again under cold water and, using your hands, try to remove as much of the thin outer layer of skin as possible.

4. In a large pot of boiling water, cook only the octopus tentacles for 10 seconds, and then quickly remove them. Repeat this process 5–6 times to make the tentacles curl and look nicer on the finished plate. Reserve the tentacles. Then add the carrots and celery to the pot with the rest of the octopus and cook over medium heat for at least 30 minutes, skimming off any foam that rises to the top of pot.

5. Remove the octopus and veggies from the water. Discard the veggies and let the octopus cool down. Using the same boiling water, cook the squid for 10 minutes, and then remove and set it aside. Then do the same with the shrimp, cooking them in the same boiling water for 3 minutes, and then removing and setting them aside.

6. In a large stockpot, heat 1 tablespoon (15ml) of the olive oil and sauté one tablespoon (5g) garlic. Add the clams and mussels to the pot and cook them, with the lid on, until they completely open. Then remove the pot from the heat and let it cool.

7. Once the pot is cool, remove the meat from the clam and mussel shells (or leave them intact, if you prefer). Transfer them to a big mixing bowl. Slice the squid and octopus, and add them, with the shrimp, to the bowl. Mix all the seafood together and gently toss it with the remaining olive oil, the 1 tablespoon (5g) of parsley, salt and pepper to taste, and some lemon juice. Serve the seafood salad in a large bowl. Garnish with the curled octopus tentacles.

Insalata con Pollo Burro e Salvia

(BUTTER AND SAGE CHICKEN SALAD)

ONE OF MY SWEETEST MEMORIES OF CHILDHOOD IS EATING THIS SIMPLE, DELICIOUS CHICKEN DISH. MY DAD USED TO CUT THE CHICKEN INTO LITTLE SQUARES AND COOK IT WITH SOME SAGE AND BUTTER, AND MY BROTHER AND I WOULD FIGHT OVER IT. IT'S THAT GOOD!

PREP TIME: *15 minutes* | COOKING TIME: *12 minutes; 22 minutes, if you add hard-boiled egg* | SERVES: *4*

INGREDIENTS

3 boneless chicken breasts (about 1½ pounds [730g])

Flour, enough to coat the chicken (about 1 cup [125g])

2 tablespoons (30ml) extra virgin olive oil, plus more for dressing the salad

3½ ounces (100g) butter

15 sage leaves

Salt and pepper to taste

3 ounces (85g) baby spinach

2 hard-boiled eggs, sliced

Juice of 1 lemon

12 sun-dried tomatoes, sliced (optional)

INSTRUCTIONS

1. With a sharp knife, cut the chicken breasts into ½-inch (12mm) thick slices. Dredge the chicken slices in the flour to coat them completely. In a medium saucepan, heat 2 tablespoons (30ml) olive oil and melt the butter. When the saucepan is hot, place the chicken breasts in the pan and cook them for 6–7 minutes on each side. Then add the sage and salt and pepper to taste.

2. When the chicken is cooked, remove it from the pan and let it rest for 5 minutes. While the chicken is resting, toss the baby spinach, a splash of olive oil, and hard-boiled eggs in a bowl. Squeeze a little fresh lemon juice and some salt and pepper on the salad and mix it well.

3. Serve the salad with the chicken on the side. Top with sun-dried tomatoes, if desired.

Insalata Vegetariana

(VEGETARIAN SALAD)

THIS IS A VERY LIGHT AND REFRESHING SALAD, PERFECT FOR A WARM SUMMER DAY.

PREP TIME: *10 minutes* | COOKING TIME: *25 minutes* | SERVES: *4*

INGREDIENTS

12 cippolini onions

1 tablespoon (15ml) extra virgin olive oil for drizzling over the salad

1 zucchini

1 summer squash

1 eggplant

1 red bell pepper

1–2 ounces (30–60g) arugula

1 whole fresh buffalo mozzarella, diced

Salt and pepper to taste

INSTRUCTIONS

1. First, place the cippolini onions on a sheet pan. Drizzle 1 tablespoon (15ml) olive oil over the onions and bake them in the oven at 350°F (180°C) for 15–20 minutes or until they turn golden. Take them out of the oven and set them aside.

2. With a sharp knife, cut the zucchini, summer squash, eggplant, and bell pepper into long strips, and grill them over medium to high heat for about 3 minutes on each side. Chop the grilled vegetables and set them aside.

3. In a large salad bowl, toss together the arugula, grilled veggies, diced buffalo mozzarella, and salt and pepper to taste. Top the salad with the cippolini onions and a drizzle of olive oil.

PIZZAS

PIZZA IS PROBABLY THE MOST ICONIC OF ALL ITALIAN FOOD. EVERYONE KNOWS WHAT PIZZA IS! IN ITALY, YOU EAT PIZZA AT LEAST ONCE A WEEK AND I ALWAYS ENJOY MAKING IT IN OUR WOOD-FIRE PIZZA OVEN WITH MY FAMILY.

Impasto per la Pizza di Base

(BASIC PIZZA DOUGH)

PIZZA IS A CLASSIC FOOD FROM ITALY, SAID TO HAVE ORIGINATED IN CAMPANIA, IN SOUTHERN ITALY. IT IS, QUITE SIMPLY, A MIXTURE OF FLOUR, WATER, YEAST, OLIVE OIL, SALT, AND A BIT OF SUGAR. THE DOUGH IS RISEN TWICE AND COOKED IN A WOOD-FIRE OVEN FOR JUST A FEW MINUTES AT 500°F (250°C). THE DOUGH IS VERSATILE, AND CAN ALSO BE USED TO MAKE FOCACCIA AND CALZONE.

PREP TIME: *30 minutes for the dough, plus 5 hours to let it rest* | COOKING TIME: *10–12 minutes*

MAKES: *1 13 x 18-inch (33 x 46cm) pizza or 2 10-inch (25cm) pizzas*

1 cup (250ml) filtered or bottled water

3 tablespoons (45ml) extra virgin olive oil

¾ teaspoon (5g) salt

½ teaspoon (2g) white sugar

⅛ ounce (5g) fresh yeast, crumbled

3 cups (375g) all-purpose flour

INSTRUCTIONS

1. In order to make a good pizza dough, you should plan to begin the recipe at least 7 hours in advance. To begin, combine water, olive oil, salt, sugar, and fresh yeast in a mixing bowl with a hook attachment. Start mixing on first speed and slowly incorporate the flour without turning off the mixer. Continue to mix until all flour has been absorbed and the mixture looks smooth and comes off the sides of the bowl and hook attachment easily. Cover the dough with plastic wrap and place it on a flat surface, not allowing it to come into contact with any air for 10 minutes.

2. Next, take the dough out of the plastic wrap and roll it into a ball. The rolled ball should be a little over 1 pound (650g), enough to make one 13 x 18-inch (33 x 46cm) pizza or two 10-inch (25cm) pizzas.

3. Lay the ball in an airtight container and cover it up tightly with plastic wrap. Let it rest for about 5 hours. After 5 hours, your dough will double in size. Roll it into a ball once again. Cover it again, and let it rest for another 30 minutes to 1 hour so it will rise for a second time. After 30 minutes, your dough is ready to be rolled out and made into a pizza.

4. On a flat surface, sprinkle and flour the surface, then take the dough and push your palm into the side of it, rotating and kneading the dough as you form it into a circle. Always leave 1 inch (3cm) of space for your crust. Your basic pizza dough is now ready. When the dough is thin enough, spread some tomato sauce, sprinkle some mozzarella cheese, drizzle some extra virgin olive oil, and cook it at 500°F (250°C) for 10–12 minutes or until the crust is golden brown.

Pizza Margherita con Mozzarella di Bufala

(MARGHERITA PIZZA WITH BUFFALO MOZZARELLA)

BUFFALO MOZZARELLA IS CONSIDERED THE "QUEEN OF MEDITERRANEAN CUISINE" BECAUSE OF ITS VERSATILITY AND ELASTIC TEXTURE.

PREP TIME: *6 hours for dough to rise* | COOKING TIME: *5 minutes* | *Makes: 1 large (about 10–12-inch [25–30cm]) pizza or two small pizzas (each 6 inches [15cm])* | *Serves: 8*

Basic Pizza Dough (page 110)

One 15-ounce (400g) can San Marzano tomatoes

Salt to taste

4–5 tablespoons (60–75ml) extra virgin olive oil

1 whole ball (about ½ pound [230g]) fresh buffalo mozzarella, sliced

12 cherry tomatoes, halved

Handful of fresh basil

INSTRUCTIONS

1. Prepare the pizza dough (page 110).

2. Place a pizza stone in the oven on the top rack.

3. Preheat the oven to 500°F (250°C) and let it heat for at least 45 minutes.

4. When the dough is ready, prepare the pizza sauce. In a bowl, use an immersion blender to purée the tomatoes. Then, add a little salt and 4 tablespoons (60ml) of olive oil to the tomatoes and mix well. Pour the sauce into the center of the stretched dough and use the back of a large spoon or ladle to spread it evenly across the surface, stopping approximately 1 inch (3cm) from the edges.

5. Arrange the mozzarella slices on top of the sauce, then add the sliced cherry tomatoes, and finally the basil leaves. Slide the pizza onto the pizza stone. Bake the pizza for about 5 minutes or until the crust is golden brown, slightly charred, and the cheese is bubbling in places, making sure to rotate the pizza throughout the cooking time. When the pizza is done, transfer it to a cutting board, garnish it with a touch of extra virgin olive oil, and cut it into 8 slices.

Pizza Speck e Mascarpone

(PIZZA WITH SPECK AND MASCARPONE)

SPECK IS A DRY-CURED HAM, LIKE PROSCIUTTO, BUT IT IS ALSO SMOKED, IN THE TRADITION OF NORTHERN ITALY. SPECK HAMS ARE SALTED AND FRAGRANT WITH A MIXTURE OF SEASONINGS, SUCH AS PEPPER, JUNIPER, AND ROSEMARY. IN ORDER FOR THE HAM TO BE CALLED "SPECK," IT MUST MEET EUROPEAN COMMISSION STANDARDS AND CURE FOR AT LEAST TWENTY-TWO WEEKS.

PREP TIME: *8 hours with dough, 1 hour without* | COOKING TIME: *10 minutes* |
SERVES: *6 slices*

Basic Pizza Dough (page 110)

One 15-ounce (400g) can San Marzano tomatoes

Salt to taste

4 tablespoons (60ml) extra virgin olive oil

1 ball (about ½ pound [230g]) fresh buffalo mozzarella, diced into small cubes

5 teaspoons (25g) mascarpone cheese for each slice of pizza

6 slices speck

INSTRUCTIONS

1. Prepare the pizza dough (page 110).

2. Place a pizza stone on the top rack of the oven.

3. Preheat the oven to 500°F (250°C) and let it heat for at least 45 minutes.

4. When the dough is ready, prepare the pizza sauce. In a bowl, use an immersion blender to purée the tomatoes. Then, add a pinch of salt, if you like, and the olive oil to the tomatoes and mix well.

5. In another bowl, drain the diced mozzarella over a cheesecloth or chinois (a conical sieve with an extremely fine mesh), for at least 1 hour so when you make your pizza, the excess water will not make the crust soggy.

6. Pour the sauce into the center of the stretched dough and use the back of a large spoon or ladle to spread it evenly across the surface, stopping approximately 1 inch (3cm)

from the edges. Add a little bit of the strained, diced mozzarella and 5 dollops of the mascarpone, and spread it evenly across the pizza.

7. Bake the pizza for 3–4 minutes or until the crust is golden brown and the cheese is bubbling, making sure to rotate the pizza throughout the cooking time. When it's done, spread speck around the pizza evenly, transfer it to a cutting board, and cut it into 6 slices.

Pizza Quattro Stagioni

(FOUR SEASONS PIZZA)

THIS CLASSIC PIZZA GETS ITS NAME FROM THE FOUR SEASONS, EACH OF WHICH OFFERS A BOUNTY OF DELICIOUS INGREDIENTS, SOME OF WHICH ARE FEATURED HERE: OLIVES FOR SUMMER, MUSHROOMS FOR AUTUMN, HAM FOR WINTER, AND ARTICHOKES FOR SPRING.

PREP TIME: *8 hours with dough, 15 minutes without* | COOKING TIME: *15 minutes* |

SERVES: *4*

Basic Pizza Dough (page 110)

One 15-ounce (400g) can San Marzano tomatoes

Salt and pepper to taste

7 tablespoons (105ml) extra virgin olive oil, divided (four tablespoons for the tomatoes)

Mozzarella, diced into small cubes

1 garlic clove, crushed

1 sprig thyme

½ cup (60g) shiitake mushrooms, sliced

8 baby artichokes, cut into matchstick-thin strips

6 ounces (170g) black olives, sliced

5 slices prosciutto cotto or ham

INSTRUCTIONS

1. Prepare the pizza dough (page 110).

2. Place a pizza stone on the top rack of the oven

3. Preheat the oven to 500°F (250°C) and let it heat for at least 45 minutes.

4. When the dough is ready. Prepare the pizza sauce. In a bowl, use an immersion blender to purée the tomatoes. Add a pinch of salt, if you like, and 4 tablespoons (60ml) of the olive oil to the tomatoes and mix well.

5. In another bowl, drain the diced mozzarella over a cheesecloth or *chinois* (a conical sieve with an extremely fine mesh), for at least 1 hour so when you make your pizza, the excess water will not make the crust soggy.

6. Pour the sauce into the center of the stretched dough and use the back of a large spoon or ladle to spread it evenly across the surface, stopping approximately 1 inch (3cm) from the edges. Add some of the previously strained diced mozzarella and spread it evenly across the pizza.

7. In a pan, heat 3 tablespoons (45ml) of olive oil and add the crushed garlic and the sprig of thyme. Sauté for 1 minute and then toss in the shiitake mushrooms and artichokes (see page 45 for tips on how to clean them). Add a pinch of salt and pepper, to taste, and cook the mixture for 7–8 minutes over medium heat.

8. Once cooked, spread the veggies evenly around the top of the pizza and add the olives.

9. Bake the pizza for 3–4 minutes or until the crust is golden brown, making sure to rotate the pizza throughout the cooking time. When it's done, spread the prosciutto or ham slices on top of the pizza, transfer it to a cutting board, and cut it into 8 slices.

Calzone Ricotta e Salsiccia

(CALZONE WITH RICOTTA AND SAUSAGE)

THIS IS MY UNCLE VINCENZO'S GREATEST CALZONE. HE USED TO MAKE IT
DOWNSTAIRS, IN OUR SMALL, WOOD-FIRE OVEN, AT HOME, IN LUCCA. HE WOULD
THEN COME UPSTAIRS, YELLING FOR THE WHOLE FAMILY TO COME DOWN AND TRY
HIS AMAZING CREATION.

PREP TIME: *8 hours with dough, 15 minutes without* | COOKING TIME: *8 minutes* |
SERVES: *4*

INGREDIENTS

Basic Pizza Dough (page 110)

One 15-ounce (400g) can San Marzano
tomatoes

Salt and pepper to taste

3 tablespoons (45ml) extra virgin
olive oil

3½ ounces (100g) Italian sausage,
such as salsiccia

½ cup (125g) ricotta

INSTRUCTIONS

1. Prepare the pizza dough (page 110).

2. Preheat the oven to 450°F (230°C). Let it heat for at least 45 minutes.

3. When the dough is ready, prepare the sauce. In a bowl, use an immersion blender to purée the tomatoes. Add a pinch of salt and the olive oil. Heat the sauce in a saucepan.

4. Remove the sausage from the casing. Discard the casing and crumble the meat with the back of a spoon or with your fingers. Brown the sausage in a skillet over medium heat, until it is cooked through, and then transfer it to a plate to drain on paper towels.

5. In another bowl, combine the ricotta with the sausage meat and mix well. Add a pinch of salt and pepper. Spread the mixture evenly over half of the pizza dough and fold the other side on top of it. Using your fingers, press down firmly to seal the edges of the calzone. Assemble it on a pizza pan or baking sheet so you don't have to lift and move it after you've assembled the calzone and it's ready to go into the oven.

6. Bake the calzone for about 5–8 minutes or until it is crispy and golden. Be sure to rotate it throughout the cooking time. Serve with the warm tomato sauce.

Pizza alla Diavola

(MARGHERITA PIZZA WITH CALABRESE SALAMI)

CALABRESE SALAMI IS NAMED AFTER CALABRIA, A REGION IN SOUTHERN ITALY. THIS COARSELY GROUND PORK SALAMI IS MILDLY HOT BECAUSE IT'S MADE WITH A GENEROUS AMOUNT OF RED PEPPER FLAKES. ONCE IT GOES INTO THE OVEN, THE SALAMI GETS CRISPY AND ADDS A LOT OF FLAVOR TO THE PIZZA. I'VE ENJOYED EATING IT EVER SINCE I WAS A KID, AND IT'S STILL ONE OF MY FAVORITES.

PREP TIME: *8 hours with dough, 15 minutes without* | COOKING TIME: *5 minutes* | SERVES: *4*

Basic Pizza Dough (page 110)

One 15-ounce (400g) can San Marzano tomatoes

Salt and pepper to taste

4 tablespoons (60ml) extra virgin olive oil

1 ball (about ½ pound [230g]) fresh mozzarella ball, diced

5 slices Calabrese salami

Crushed red chili flakes, to taste

12 cherry tomatoes, halved

INSTRUCTIONS

1. Prepare the pizza dough (page 110).

2. Place a pizza stone on the top rack of the oven.

3. Preheat the oven to 500°F (250°C) and let it heat for at least 45 minutes.

4. When the dough is ready, prepare the pizza sauce. In a bowl, use an immersion blender to purée the tomatoes. Add a pinch of salt and 4 tablespoons (60ml) of olive oil.

5. In another bowl, drain the diced mozzarella over a cheesecloth or chinois (a conical sieve with an extremely fine mesh), for at least 1 hour so when you make your pizza, the excess water will not make the crust soggy.

6. Pour the sauce into the center of the stretched dough and use the back of a large spoon or ladle to spread it evenly across the surface, stopping approximately 1 inch (3cm) from the edges. Add the previously strained diced mozzarella and spread it

evenly across the pizza. Then add 5 slices of the Calabrese salami, the crushed red chili flakes (the amount you use depends on how spicy you would like the pizza to be), and the cherry tomatoes. Add salt and pepper to taste, but keep in mind that the salami is already salty, peppery, and spicy so, for a milder pizza, do not add any extra seasonings.

7. Bake the pizza for 3–4 minutes or until the crust is golden brown, making sure to rotate the pizza throughout the cooking time.

Focaccina Prosciutto Cotto e Mozzarella

(FOCACCIA WITH HAM AND FRESH MOZZARELLA)

I REMEMBER MY DAD MAKING THIS FOCACCIA AT HOME IN ITALY, WHEN MY BROTHER AND I WERE GROWING UP. THIS RECIPE FOR OVEN-BAKED BREAD IS LIKE MAKING A PIZZA WITHOUT ANY TOMATO SAUCE. IN FACT, THE FIRST PIZZAS WERE WHITE, MADE WITH JUST A LITTLE LARD, BASIL LEAVES, CHEESE, AND PEPPER.

PREP TIME: *8 hours with dough, 15 minutes without* | COOKING TIME: *5 minutes* | SERVES: *4*

Basic Pizza Dough (page 110)

3 tablespoons (45ml) extra virgin olive oil

4 sprigs rosemary, removed from stem

1 fresh buffalo mozzarella ball, cut into 4 slices

5 slices prosciutto cotto or ham

Salt and pepper to taste

INSTRUCTIONS

1. Prepare the pizza dough (page 110).

2. Preheat the oven to 500°F (250°C). Let it heat for at least 45 minutes.

3. Flatten and thin out the dough the same way you would if you were making a pizza. Now drizzle the olive oil on top and sprinkle the rosemary sprigs evenly over it. Add the mozzarella and prosciutto slices (or other ham, if you're using it). Sprinkle a little salt and pepper to taste.

4. Bake the focaccia for about 3–4 minutes or until it is golden, making sure to rotate it in the oven throughout the cooking time.

Pizza Caprese

(WHITE PIZZA CAPRESE STYLE WITH PESTO)

THIS PIZZA COMES FROM CAPRI, IN THE SOUTH OF ITALY. IT SHOWCASES SOME
OF THE FINEST INGREDIENTS OF ITALIAN AND MEDITERRANEAN CUISINE—BASIL,
MOZZARELLA, AND RED TOMATOES—WHICH JUST HAPPEN TO BE THE COLORS OF THE
GREEN, WHITE, AND RED ITALIAN FLAG.

PREP TIME: *8 hours with dough, 10 minutes without* | COOKING TIME: *5 minutes* |
SERVES: *4*

INGREDIENTS

Basic Pizza Dough (page 110)

2–3 teaspoons (5–10g) pesto for each
slice (page 29)

1 fresh buffalo mozzarella ball, cut
into 4 slices

16 fresh basil leaves

4–5 heirloom tomatoes, sliced

Salt and pepper to taste

1 tablespoon (15ml) extra virgin
olive oil

INSTRUCTIONS

1. Prepare the pizza dough (page 110).

2. Prepare the pesto (page 29).

3. Place a pizza stone on the top rack of the oven.

4. Preheat the oven to 500°F (250°C) and let it heat for at least 45 minutes.

5. When the dough is ready, spoon the pesto onto the stretched dough and use
the back of the spoon to spread it evenly across the surface, stopping approximately
1 inch (3cm) from the edges.

6. Bake the pizza for about 3–4 minutes or until the pizza is golden, making sure
to rotate it throughout the cooking time.

7. Take the pizza out of the oven and top it with the slices of fresh mozzarella. Put 2
basil leaves, and then a slice of heirloom tomato on top of each slice of mozzarella, until
the entire pizza is covered. Add salt and pepper to taste and drizzle with some olive oil.

Pizza Bresaola, Rucola e Burrata

(PIZZA WITH BRESAOLA, ARUGULA, AND BURRATA CHEESE)

BRESAOLA OR, IN ITALIAN DIALECT, BRISAOLA, IS AN AIR-DRIED, SALTED BEEF THAT ORIGINATED IN VALTELLINA, A VALLEY IN THE ALPS OF NORTHERN ITALY'S LOMBARDY REGION. BRESAOLA IS MADE FROM THE TOP ROUND OF BEEF AND IS AGED FOR A COUPLE OF MONTHS UNTIL IT BECOMES HARD AND TURNS A DEEP RED COLOR. THE FLAVOR OF THIS LEAN, TENDER BEEF IS SWEET AND AROMATIC.

PREP TIME: *8 hours with dough, 15 minutes without* | COOKING TIME: *5 minutes* |

SERVES: *4*

Basic Pizza Dough (page 110)

One 15-ounce (400g) can San Marzano
  tomatoes

Salt and pepper to taste

5 tablespoons (75ml) extra virgin
  olive oil

16 slices bresaola

1 ball (about ½ pound [230g]) burrata
  cheese

3 ounces (85g) arugula

INSTRUCTIONS

1. Prepare the pizza dough (page 110).

2. Place a pizza stone on the top rack of the oven.

3. Preheat the oven to 500°F (250°C) and let it heat for at least 45 minutes.

4. When the dough is ready, prepare the pizza sauce. In a bowl, use an immersion blender to purée the tomatoes. Add a pinch of salt and 4 tablespoons (60ml) of olive oil. With a large spoon or a ladle, pour the sauce in the center and spread it outward toward the crust, leaving 1 inch (3cm) for the crust.

5. Bake the pizza for about 3–4 minutes or until the pizza is golden, making sure to rotate it throughout the cooking time.

6. Once cooked, take the pizza out of the oven and garnish the pie with the slices of bresaola, the burrata, and the arugula, until the entire pizza is covered. Finish with a sprinkle of salt and pepper, to taste, and a generous splash of olive oil.

Pizza Mari e Monti

(SEA AND MOUNTAIN PIZZA)

THE NAME OF THIS PIZZA PERFECTLY DESCRIBES THE LOCATION OF MY HOMETOWN: LUCCA LIES BETWEEN THE SEA AND THE MOUNTAINS, APPROXIMATELY 20 MINUTES EACH WAY. IF YOU HAVE EXTRA CLAMS, MUSSELS, AND MUSHROOMS, JUST ADD SOME GARLIC AND THE LEFTOVER TOMATOES FROM THE PIZZA, AND MAKE A TOMATO-SEAFOOD SAUCE FOR FRESH PASTA THE NEXT DAY.

PREP TIME: *7 hours, 20 minutes* | COOKING TIME: *8 hours, 8 minutes* | SERVES: *4*

Basic Pizza Dough (page 110)

One 15-ounce (400g) can San Marzano tomatoes

Pinch of salt

4 tablespoons (60ml) extra virgin olive oil, divided

1 fresh mozzarella ball (about ½ pound [230g]), diced into small cubes

½ pound (230g) clams

½ pound (230g) mussels

3 garlic cloves, minced

Fresh chopped parsley, for garnish

½ pound (230g) button mushrooms, sliced

INSTRUCTIONS

1. Prepare the pizza dough (page 110).

2. Place a pizza stone on the top rack of the oven.

3. Preheat the oven to 500°F (250°C) and let it heat for at least 45 minutes.

4. When the dough is ready, prepare the pizza sauce. In a bowl, use an immersion blender to purée the tomatoes. Add a pinch of salt and 3 tablespoons (45ml) olive oil.

5. In another bowl, drain the diced mozzarella over a cheesecloth or chinois (a conical sieve with an extremely fine mesh), for at least 1 hour so when you make your pizza, the excess water will not make the crust soggy.

6. Thoroughly rinse the clams and mussels, cleaning the outer shell with a small brush to remove any dirt or sand. Pull off the "beard" (the sticky fibers) that emerge from the mussel shells, and then rinse the mussels again under cold water. Discard any mussels or clams that are damaged or already open. In a large pot, heat a tablespoon of the olive oil over medium heat and sauté the garlic. Add the clams and mussels to the pot and cook them with the lid on until they completely open, then take the pan off the heat and let it cool. Once the pan is cool, take the clams and mussels out of the shells.

7. Pour the sauce into the center of the stretched dough and use the back of a large spoon or ladle to spread it evenly across the surface, stopping approximately 1 inch (3cm) from the edges. Add some of the previously strained diced mozzarella and spread it evenly on the pizza. Add the mushrooms.

8. Bake the pizza for about 3–4 minutes or until the pizza is golden, making sure to rotate it throughout the cooking time. When the pizza is done, garnish it with the parsley.

CONTORNI

(SIDES)

AS THE WORD IS DEFINED IN ITALIAN, CONTORNI MEANS "OUTLINE," OR "ON THE SIDE" OF OTHER THINGS. IN A CULINARY CONTEXT, CONTORNI ARE SIDE DISHES THAT LITERALLY GO NEXT TO THE ENTRÉE, AND ARE MEANT TO COMPLEMENT AND BALANCE THE ACCOMPANYING DISH.

Zucchini al Pomodoro

(ZUCCHINI WITH TOMATO SAUCE)

YOU CAN PREPARE THIS SIDE DISH WITH MANY DIFFERENT VEGETABLES, BUT MY DAD ALWAYS MAKES IT WITH ZUCCHINI OR ZUCCHINI BLOSSOMS. IT'S AN EASY SIDE TO WHIP UP, VERY INEXPENSIVE, AND REALLY GOOD!

PREP TIME: *10 minutes* | COOKING TIME: *25 minutes* | SERVES: *4*

1 white onion

4–5 medium zucchini

4–5 tablespoons (60–75ml) extra
   virgin olive oil

1 pinch crushed red pepper

Salt and pepper to taste

One 15-ounce (400g) can crushed
   tomatoes

12 basil leaves

INSTRUCTIONS

1. On a cutting board, slice the onion thin and set it aside. Next, dice the zucchini.

2. In a large nonstick saucepan, heat 1 tablespoon (15ml) of the olive oil. Once the pan is hot, add the onion and crushed red pepper. Sauté the onion for about 5 minutes, or until it's golden and translucent. Add the zucchini and a pinch of salt and cook for another 5 minutes.

3. Add the crushed tomatoes to the saucepan and cook, covered, over medium heat for 15–20 minutes, stirring every few minutes. After 10 minutes, add the basil leaves and continue to cook until the tomatoes start to reduce and thicken to a sauce. Serve the dish hot, as a side for any meat or pork dish.

Patate Arrosto

(ROASTED POTATOES)

ROASTED POTATOES ARE THE PERFECT SIDE FOR BOTH SEAFOOD AND MEAT. THEY ARE VERY EASY TO MAKE, WHILE YOU'RE WORKING ON SOMETHING ELSE, AND THE OVEN DOES THE REST OF THE JOB.

PREP TIME: *10 minutes* | COOKING TIME: *55 minutes* | SERVES: *4*

2 pounds (1kg) potatoes, cut into small cubes

2–3 garlic cloves

4 sprigs rosemary

1–2 sprigs sage

2 tablespoons extra virgin olive oil, plus some to drizzle over the potatoes

Salt and pepper to taste

INSTRUCTIONS

1. Peel the potatoes. To remove as much starch as possible, rinse the peeled potatoes in a large bowl of cold water until it runs clear. Alternatively, you can let the potatoes soak in cold water and keep changing the water until it is no longer cloudy and stays clear. Rinsing the potatoes to remove the starch will ensure that the potatoes get crunchy when they're cooked.

2. Preheat the oven to 450°F (230°C).

3. Fill a medium pot with cold water and bring it to a boil before adding the potatoes. Cook the potatoes over medium-high heat for 4–5 minutes. Remove them from the water and let them cool in another bowl.

4. Meanwhile, finely chop the garlic and the fresh herbs. Mix them into the potatoes with 2 tablespoons of (30ml) olive oil and a pinch of salt and pepper.

5. Spread the potatoes evenly, in a single layer, on a sheet pan and drizzle them with a bit of the olive oil.

6. Roast the potatoes for about 35–40 minutes or until crunchy.

Sformato di Cavolfiore

THIS RECIPE COMES FROM MY GREAT-AUNT MAGDA, WHO PASSED AWAY ABOUT A YEAR AGO. SHE LIVED WITH MY FAMILY FROM THE TIME I WAS BORN, AND, TO ME, SHE WAS LIKE A GRANDMA. SHE WOULD MAKE FOOD FOR MY BROTHER AND ME EVERY DAY WHEN MY PARENTS WEREN'T AT HOME. ONE OF HER FAVORITE DISHES WAS THIS ONE. IT'S CREAMY ON THE INSIDE, CRUNCHY ON THE OUTSIDE, AND HAS AMAZING FLAVORS!

PREP TIME: *20 minutes* | COOKING TIME: *45 minutes* | SERVES: *4*

1 head cauliflower, cut into pieces

1¼ cups (300ml) milk

6 tablespoons (85g) butter, plus more for buttering the pan

4 eggs

½ cup (60g) bread crumbs, plus more for sprinkling on top of the casserole

½ cup (40g) parmigiano, grated

Salt to taste

INSTRUCTIONS

1. Fill a large pot with cool water and bring it to a boil. Cook the cauliflower over medium heat for about 10–12 minutes.

2. Preheat the oven to 375°F (190°C).

3. Drain the cauliflower and transfer it to a large bowl. With an immersion blender, blend the cauliflower, while adding the milk.

4. Add the butter, eggs, ½ cup (60g) bread crumbs, parmigiano, and a pinch of salt.

5. Lightly butter a 2-quart (2L) casserole dish or pan and pour the mixture inside. Sprinkle more bread crumbs on top and bake uncovered for about 40 minutes. Serve hot!

Verdure Fritte con Pastella

THIS IS A QUICK AND EASY SIDE DISH FOR JUST ABOUT ANY RECIPE. PAIR IT WITH CHICKEN OR BEEF, OR EVEN EAT ON ITS OWN.

PREP TIME: *15 minutes* | COOKING TIME: *10 minutes* | SERVES: *4*

2 eggs

Salt to taste

1 cup (240ml) cold milk

1 cup (125g) flour, sifted

Vegetable oil (enough to deep-fry vegetables)

4 zucchini, julienned

4 carrots, julienned

1 onion, sliced thin or round

1 cup (125g) cauliflower, chopped into florets

1 cup (125g) broccoli florets

INSTRUCTIONS

1. To make the batter: Separate the yolks and egg whites. In a bowl, whip the egg whites until you get stiff peaks. Set the bowl aside.

2. Whisk the yolks with a pinch of salt in a separate bowl. Then add the milk while continuously whisking. Start adding the flour a little bit at a time, while continuously whisking to prevent any lumps from forming. Gently fold the egg whites into the mixture, so they don't lose the air whipped inside.

3. For deep-frying the vegetables: In a large bowl, mix together the zucchini, carrots, onion, cauliflower, and broccoli, and pat them dry. Pour the vegetable oil into a deep cast-iron skillet, Dutch oven, or heavy aluminum pot until it is at least 1 inch (2.5cm) deep. Heat the oil to 350°F (180°C).

4. Dip the vegetables in the batter, coating them well, and frying them at 350°F (180°C) for a few minutes until they're golden. Use a thermometer to check the temperature of the oil to make sure it doesn't get too hot and burn. Once the veggies are golden, remove them from the oil and lay them on a plate lined with paper towels to soak up any excess oil. Add salt to taste. Serve immediately, while they're hot and crispy.

Fagioli all'Uccelletto

(BEANS WITH TOMATO AND SAGE SAUCE)

THIS BEAN DISH IS A CLASSIC OF TUSCAN CUISINE. THE NAME IS BELIEVED TO COME FROM THE HERBS AND BASE SAUCE THAT WAS USED TO COOK MANY DIFFERENT BIRDS DURING THE HUNTING SEASON. THE TERM *UCCELLETTI* MEANS "SMALL BIRDS," BUT I CAN ASSURE YOU, THERE ARE NO BIRDS IN THIS DISH!

PREP TIME: *24 hours, 5 minutes* | COOKING TIME: *40 minutes* | SERVES: *4*

INGREDIENTS

1¼ cups (300g) dried cannellini beans

5 tablespoons (75ml) extra virgin olive oil

2–3 garlic cloves, crushed

1 sprig sage

¾ pound (350g) peeled tomatoes, puréed

Salt and pepper to taste

Sage leaf, for garnish

INSTRUCTIONS

1. Soak the cannellini beans overnight in cold water. The next day, drain the beans and put them in a large stockpot. Cover the beans with fresh water, plus an extra 2 inches (5cm) or more, and bring to a boil. Reduce the heat and let the beans simmer gently over low heat for 25–30 minutes. You want to cook the beans slowly until they're soft, without having them break apart.

2. In a small, nonstick pot, heat about 1 tablespoon (15ml) of the olive oil, then add garlic and the sprig of sage and sauté for a few minutes on low heat so that the oil absorbs all the flavors of the garlic and sage. Now add the tomato purée and a pinch of salt and pepper. Let the mixture cook until it thickens into a sauce. Add the beans and cook for another 10–15 minutes.

3. Serve the beans in a terra-cotta bowl garnished with a crispy sage leaf.

Piselli con Pancetta e Cipolla

(PEAS WITH PANCETTA AND ONIONS)

PEAS ARE ANY EASY SIDE DISH TO MAKE AND GO NICELY WITH FISH OR CHICKEN. WHEN I HAVE NO TIME TO COOK AND NEED TO PREPARE SOMETHING QUICKLY, THIS IS MY GO-TO RECIPE.

PREP TIME: *10 minutes* | COOKING TIME: *20 minutes* | SERVES: *4*

1 cup (400g) frozen peas

3 tablespoons (45ml) extra virgin olive oil

1 medium-size onion, sliced thin

3 ounces (85g) pancetta, cubed

Salt and pepper to taste

INSTRUCTIONS

1. In a small saucepan, bring some water to a boil and cook the peas for about 5 minutes. Remove the pan from the heat and drain the peas.

2. Meanwhile, in another saucepan, heat the olive oil, then add the onions and cook them until they're golden and translucent. Add the pancetta and cook it until it gets crispy. Add the peas. Cook the mixture for 10 more minutes on low to medium heat, remembering to stir it occasionally. Add salt and pepper to taste.

3. Serve the peas as a side dish to your favorite meat entrée!

Finocchi Gratinati

(FENNEL AU GRATIN)

IN THIS RECIPE, FENNEL IS PREPARED WITH BÉCHAMEL SAUCE AND GRATED
PARMIGIANO, BUT YOU CAN ALSO USE OTHER VEGETABLES, LIKE BROCCOLI OR
CAULIFLOWER. IT'LL TASTE JUST AS GOOD, AND MAKES A GREAT ACCOMPANIMENT
TO FISH AND LEAN MEATS.

PREP TIME: *20 minutes* | COOKING TIME: *50 minutes* | SERVES: *4*

INGREDIENTS

4 medium-size fennel bulbs

4 tablespoons (60g) butter, divided

¼ cup (30g) flour

1¼ cups (300ml) milk

Pinch of ground nutmeg

2 tablespoons (30ml) extra virgin olive oil

Salt to taste

½ cup (40g) parmigiano, grated

Fresh ground pepper, to taste

INSTRUCTIONS

1. Preheat the oven to 375°F (190°C).

2. Remove the stalks from each fennel bulb. Cut the bulbs in half lengthwise and then slice them in half again. Remove the core. Continue halving the pieces until you have a total of 8. Now cook them in a large pot of boiling water for 10–12 minutes.

3. In the meantime, in a small saucepan, melt 2 tablespoons (30g) butter, then take the pan off the heat and add the flour. Whisk everything together and mix well to create a roux. Whisk in the milk, return the pot to the heat, and continue cooking until the mixture starts to thicken. Continue to whisk and add the nutmeg.

4. In a large saucepan, heat the olive oil and sauté the boiled fennel. Add 2 tablespoons (30g) butter. Cook over medium-low heat for 4–5 minutes until the fennel starts to caramelize, and then add a little salt to taste.

5. When the fennel wedges have finished cooking in the pan, transfer them to a gratin or other baking dish and pour the sauce from the pan on top. Sprinkle over the grated parmigiano and bake uncovered for about 20 minutes, or until the fennel and grated cheese are nice and golden. Let the dish cool for 5 minutes before serving.

PART 2
DOLCE (SWEET)

DOLCE
(DESSERTS)

DESSERTS HAVE BEEN A SWEET PART OF MY LIFE EVER SINCE I WAS A KID. HERE YOU'LL LEARN HOW TO MAKE ALL THE ITALIAN DESSERTS I GREW UP EATING, THANKS TO MY NONNA AND MAMMA!

Pan di Spagna

(SPONGE CAKE)

FROM THE MOMENT OF ITS CREATION BY AN ITALIAN CHEF, *PAN DI SPAGNA* HAS BECOME A FIXTURE IN EVERYDAY BAKING IN ITALY. ITS APPEARANCE, FRAGRANCE, AND TEXTURE—GOLD-COLORED, DELICATELY PERFUMED, AND SOFTLY SPONGY—ARE AS DISTINCTIVE AS ITS TASTE.

PREP TIME: *20 minutes* | COOKING TIME: *35 minutes* | SERVES: *6*

1 vanilla bean, seeds scraped out

5 eggs

Pinch of salt

¾ cup (150g) sugar

Zest of 1 orange (optional)

½ cup (75g) cake flour

½ cup (75g) potato starch

INSTRUCTIONS

1. Preheat the oven to 350°F (180°C).

2. Cut the vanilla bean and remove the seeds.

3. Combine the eggs, salt, sugar, vanilla bean seeds, and orange zest, if using. In the bowl of an electric stand mixer, fitted with a whisk attachment, beat the mixture for at least 10 minutes at medium speed until it is light and fluffy.

4. Sift the flour and potato starch over the egg mixture before folding it in very carefully with a rubber spatula from the bottom to the top, being careful not to beat the air out of the mixture.

5. Grease and flour a 9-inch (23cm) round baking pan, if you want a tall sponge cake (otherwise use a 10-inch [25cm] round pan for a larger, slightly flatter cake) and pour in the mixture. Gently even out the batter with an offset spatula. Bake the cake until the top is golden brown, 30–35 minutes.

6. Once the sponge cake is done, remove it from the oven and let it cool. Remove the cake from the pan and serve it, as is, or stuff it with one of your favorite fillings.

Pasta Frolla

(BASIC SHORTBREAD DOUGH)

SHORTBREAD IS A VERSATILE BASE FOR ANY NUMBER OF EXCELLENT DESSERTS. IT IS THE CORNERSTONE OF PASTRY MAKING AND VERY SIMPLE TO LEARN. ONCE YOU'VE MASTERED THE SIMPLE STEPS BELOW, YOU'LL BE READY TO MAKE—AND ENJOY—MANY DELICIOUS DESSERTS.

PREP TIME: *10 minutes* | COOKING TIME: *15 minutes* | SERVES: *4*

8½ ounces (240g) butter

1 cup (150g) powdered sugar

2 egg yolks

2¾ cups (360g) flour

Zest of ½ lemon

1 vanilla bean, seeds scraped out

INSTRUCTIONS

1. With a beater attachment on an electric stand mixer, combine the butter and powdered sugar, mixing at the lowest speed.

2. Once the butter and sugar are fully combined, add the egg yolks. Incorporate the flour all at once and mix it in the bowl of the mixer until the batter is smooth. Flavor the pastry with the lemon zest and vanilla bean seeds.

3. Turn out the dough onto a work surface and knead it quickly to make sure all the ingredients are combined. Form the dough into two equal-sized disks, wrap them in wax paper, and put them in the fridge to chill. It takes 30 minutes to 1 hour for the shortbread to chill, but overnight is preferable.

Genoise

(BASIC SPONGE CAKE)

WITH THIS BASIC RECIPE, YOU CAN CREATE A THIN LAYER OF SPONGE CAKE FOR COUNTLESS APPLICATIONS. THE THINNESS OF THE SPONGE GIVES YOU THE OPTION OF FILLING AND ROLLING THE CAKE OR USING IT TO BUILD A LAYERED CAKE.

PREP TIME: *15 minutes* | COOKING TIME: *5 minutes* | SERVES: *6*

Vegetable oil for greasing the pan

5 eggs at room temperature

¾ cup (175g) sugar

1 vanilla bean, seeds scraped out

Pinch of salt

¾ cup (100g) all-purpose flour

¼ cup (80g) butter, melted

INSTRUCTIONS

1. Preheat the oven to 450°F (230°C). Oil a baking sheet pan and line it with parchment paper.

2. Crack the eggs into the bowl of an electric stand mixer fitted with a whisk attachment. Add the sugar, vanilla bean seeds, and salt. Mix at medium to high speed for at least 8 minutes, while gently warming the outside of the bowl with a kitchen blowtorch (like the kind you'd use to caramelize sugar when you're making crème brûlée), being very careful not to overheat or burn the batter or expose the torch to the heat or open flames. (Another approach is to use the eggs at room temperature.) The warmth will allow the ingredients in the bowl to rise and incorporate air, which is the most important part of creating a light, airy sponge.

3. Sift the flour into the egg mixture, gently folding it in. Place about 10 percent of the batter in a separate bowl and combine it with the melted butter (the butter should be liquefied, but not hot). Once the butter is thoroughly mixed in, fold it back into the bowl with the rest of the batter.

4. Pour the batter onto the prepared baking sheet. Using an offset spatula, spread the sponge batter into a thin layer and bake for 4–5 minutes or until golden brown.

Pan di Spagna al Cioccolato

CHOCOLATE SPONGE CAKE IS ONE OF MANY VARIATIONS OF THE TRADITIONAL SPONGE (SEE *GENOISE* [BASIC SPONGE CAKE], PAGE 154). IT'S SWEET, TASTY, AND WIDELY USED IN PASTRY MAKING. CHOCOLATE SPONGE CAKE IS THE IDEAL BASE FOR DELICIOUS CAKES THAT CAN BE FILLED WITH ANY TYPE OF CREAM, SUCH AS *CREMA DIPLOMATICA* (DIPLOMAT CUSTARD, PAGE 169), WHICH NICELY COMPLEMENTS THE FLAVOR OF THE CHOCOLATE.

PREP TIME: *15 minutes* | COOKING TIME: *30 minutes* | SERVES: *6*

12 egg yolks	8 egg whites
1 cup (200g) sugar	⅓ cup (50g) all-purpose flour, sifted
Zest of ½ lemon	⅓ cup (50g) potato starch
1 vanilla bean, seeds scraped out	⅓ cup (50g) cocoa powder
Pinch of salt	8 tablespoons (110g) unsalted butter, melted, plus more for buttering the pan
¼ cup (50g) sugar	

INSTRUCTIONS

1. Preheat the convection oven to 350°F (180°C). Butter a 9-inch (23cm) round baking pan.

2. In the bowl of an electric stand mixer, fitted with a whisk attachment, beat the egg yolks at high speed. With the mixer on, gradually add 1 cup (200g) of sugar, lemon zest, vanilla bean seeds, and salt, and continue beating until the mixture is fluffy.

3. In a separate bowl whip ¼ cup (50g) of sugar and the egg whites until the mixture is creamy. Gently fold the egg whites into the egg-yolk mixture.

4. In another bowl, sift the flour, potato starch, and cocoa powder. Very gently put ⅓ of this dry ingredient mixture into the egg mixture, then slowly add ⅓ more at a time.

5. Take about 1/10 of the mixture and gently incorporate it into the melted butter. Then fold this mixture back into the rest of the batter.

6. Pour the batter into the prepared baking pan and bake right away for 25–30 minutes in a convection oven.

Pâte à Choux

(BASIC CREAM PUFF PASTRY)

THIS IS ONE OF MY FAVORITE RECIPES BECAUSE IT MAKES THE PERFECT BASE FOR
PROFITEROLES (PAGE 215) AND MANY OTHER DELICIOUS DESSERTS. ALL THE CREDIT
GOES TO THE LIGHT AND DELICATE CHOUX PASTRY, A BASIC PREPARATION—AND A
NEUTRAL FORM—THAT CAN BE FILLED WITH DELICIOUS CREAMS, BOTH SWEET AND
SAVORY. CHOUX PASTRY GETS ITS NAME FROM THE FRENCH WORD FOR "CABBAGES,"
BECAUSE, AS THE PASTRY PUFFS UP IN THE OVEN, IT TAKES ON THE SHAPE OF A
BRUSSELS SPROUT.

PREP TIME: *30 minutes* | COOKING TIME: *15 minutes* | SERVES: *10–12 (Makes
approximately 20 cream puffs)*

Vegetable oil, for greasing the pan	Pinch of salt
1 cup (240ml) water	¾ cup (90g) all-purpose flour
8 tablespoons (110g) unsalted butter, cubed	4 large eggs

INSTRUCTIONS

1. Preheat the oven to 350°F (200°C). With a brush, lightly grease a baking sheet
with oil.

2. Bring the water, butter, and salt to a boil in a medium saucepan. Add the flour all
at once. Cook the mixture over low heat, stirring briskly for 1–2 minutes, or until the
mixture forms a ball and begins to pull away from the sides of the saucepan.

3. Transfer the mixture to the bowl of an electric stand mixer, fitted with the paddle
attachment. Beating the mixture on low, incorporate the eggs slowly, one at a time,
until the mixture is well combined.

4. While it's still warm (but not hot), spoon the *choux* paste into a pastry bag fitted
with a ½-inch (12mm) plain tip. Pipe the pastry into circles about 1 inch (3cm) high and
a little over 1 inch tall, onto the baking sheet. Bake the puffs for 30 minutes, or until
they are golden brown and feel hollow. Transfer the baking sheet to a cooling rack and
allow the puffs to cool to room temperature. Now your *pâte à choux* are ready to make
éclairs, cream puffs, and so many other delicious desserts!

Gluten-Free Chocolate Sponge Cake

A CHOCOLATE SPONGE CAKE WITHOUT ANY GLUTEN NEEDS SOMETHING TO KEEP IT AIRY AND LIGHT. IN THIS RECIPE, THE AIR, CREATED BY BEATING THE EGGS, GIVES THE SPONGE ITS HEIGHT. TO MAKE THIS WORK, AVOID OVERBEATING THE EGGS, AND DELICATELY, GENTLY, FOLD IN ALL THE OTHER INGREDIENTS. TOP THE CAKE WITH YOUR FAVORITE FROSTING.

PREP TIME: *20 minutes* | COOKING TIME: *20–30 minutes* | SERVES: *8*

INGREDIENTS

2 egg yolks

½ cup (100g) sugar

5 tablespoons (70g) unsalted butter

12 ounces (350g) dark chocolate

9 egg whites

INSTRUCTIONS

1. Preheat the oven to 350°F (180°C). Grease an 8-inch (20cm) round pan (or a 9-inch [23cm] round pan, if you want a flatter cake).

2. Place the egg yolks and sugar in the bowl of an electric stand mixer, fitted with a whisk attachment, and thoroughly blend the ingredients. You may also use a handheld mixer. Beat the mixture on medium speed for about 5 minutes until it is creamy, airy, and light-colored.

3. Put the butter and dark chocolate into a heavy-bottomed saucepan and melt over medium heat, constantly stirring to blend the ingredients. Once they are combined, take the pan off the heat and allow the butter-and-chocolate mixture to cool slightly. Now stir the egg-yolk mixture into the butter-and-chocolate mixture. Set it aside.

4. Using an electric stand mixer, fitted with a whisk attachment, or a handheld mixer, beat the egg whites until stiff peaks form.

5. Slowly and gently fold the egg whites into the egg yolk–butter–chocolate mixture. Pour the batter into the greased pan and bake for 20–30 minutes.

Biscotti al Cioccolato

(CHOCOLATE BISCOTTI)

THIS IS ONE OF THE MOST RENOWNED COOKIES IN ITALY. BECAUSE THERE ARE SO MANY RECIPES FOR BISCOTTI, THIS VARIATION KEEPS IT SIMPLE AND DELICIOUS WITH A COMBINATION OF CHOCOLATE AND PISTACHIOS.

PREP TIME: *30 minutes* | COOKING TIME: *35 minutes* | SERVES: *6–8 (Makes approximately 30 biscotti)*

FOR THE BISCOTTI

1 cup (120g) pistachios, shelled

8 tablespoons (110g) unsalted butter

1 cup (200g) sugar

2 eggs

½ cup (60g) cocoa powder

1 teaspoon (5ml) honey

Pinch of salt

1 teaspoon (2.5g) baking powder

2 cups (250g) all-purpose flour

¾ cup (100g) dark chocolate chips

FOR THE TOPPING

1 whole egg, beaten

Sugar for sprinkling

INSTRUCTIONS

1. Preheat the oven to 350°F (180°C).

2. Rinse the pistachios and then scatter them over a baking sheet. Bake the nuts for 8–10 minutes at 350°F (180°C) until they're nicely toasted and aromatic. Remove the baking sheet from the oven and let the pistachios cool.

3. In a bowl, place the butter, sugar, eggs, cocoa powder, honey, salt, baking powder, and flour. Slowly mix together all the ingredients, incorporating them into a batter. Once they are thoroughly blended, add the chocolate chips and pistachio nuts.

4. Now comes the fun part. Take a piece of the dough, and, on a lightly floured surface, create a long sausage. Transfer the dough to a clean baking sheet and flatten the dough evenly to create a long loaf shape. With a pastry brush, brush the top of the dough with the beaten egg and sprinkle it with a little granulated sugar. Bake the loaf for about 15 minutes. When it's golden, remove it from the oven and let it cool on a wire rack for 15 minutes or so.

5. When the dough is cool, place it on a cutting board and cut it into ¾-inch (2cm) thick slices at a 30-degree angle. Transfer the slices to the baking sheet, with one of the cut sides facing up. Put the baking sheet back in the oven and bake the biscotti again for no more than 5 minutes (I like my chocolate biscotti a bit soft, so I bake them for only 2 more minutes). When they're cool, store the biscotti in an airtight container at room temperature for up to a month.

Sablés

(SANDIES)

THESE SHORTBREAD COOKIES ARE DELICIOUS. THEY ARE MADE OF A MIXTURE OF BUTTER (WHICH MUST BE OF EXCELLENT QUALITY), SUGAR, AND FLOUR—AND NO EGGS—WHICH MAKES FOR A COOKIE WITH A CRUMBLY TEXTURE, AS THE NAME SUGGESTS (SABLÉ MEANS "SAND" IN FRENCH). THESE COOKIES CAN BE FLAVORED WITH CINNAMON AND OTHER SPICES, OR PREPARED SIMPLY WITH SALTED BUTTER TO CREATE A CONTRAST OF SWEET AND SALTY. TRULY UNIQUE!

PREP TIME: *15 minutes* | COOKING TIME: *20 minutes* | SERVES: *6–8.*

FOR THE COOKIES

8 tablespoons (110g) unsalted butter

1⅓ cups (160g) all-purpose flour

1 vanilla bean, seeds scraped out

Zest of ½ lemon

Zest of ½ orange

Pinch of salt

2 egg yolks

½ cup (80g) granulated sugar, plus extra for sprinkling

INSTRUCTIONS

1. Preheat the oven to 350°F (180°C). Line a baking sheet with parchment paper.

2. In the bowl of a stand mixer, fitted with a beater attachment, combine the butter, flour, vanilla bean seeds, lemon zest, orange zest, and salt. Then add the egg yolks. Finish by adding the granulated sugar. Once the mixture is well combined, wrap it in plastic wrap and refrigerate for about 2 hours.

3. After the dough has chilled for 30 minutes–1 hour, roll it out on a clean work surface and form it into a long sausage shape about 3 inches (8cm) in diameter. Next, cut the dough into round slices. Place the slices on the baking sheet. Sprinkle them lightly with granulated sugar.

4. Bake the cookies for 20 minutes, until they are pale gold.

Crema Pasticcera

(VANILLA CUSTARD)

WHEN MY BROTHER AND I WERE LITTLE KIDS, MY MOM MADE FRESH VANILLA CUSTARD—WITH MILK AND EGGS FROM OUR NEIGHBOR'S FARM—JUST FOR US. SERVE THIS SWEET AND SIMPLE CUSTARD IN A COFFEE MUG AND ENJOY IT ON A TERRACE, IDEALLY WITH A VIEW OF MOUNTAINS AND FIELDS.

PREP TIME: *15 minutes* | COOKING TIME: *10 minutes* | SERVES: *8*

INGREDIENTS

3¾ cups (900 ml) milk

½ cup (100ml) heavy whipping cream

1 vanilla bean, seeds scraped out

1¼ cups (250g) sugar

10 (240g) egg yolks

½ cup (100g) sugar

¾ cup (100g) all-purpose flour

INSTRUCTIONS

1. Pour the milk and heavy whipping cream into a large saucepan. Add the vanilla bean seeds and 1¼ cups (250g) sugar to the saucepan, and bring the mixture to a boil. Then reduce the heat and stir until the sugar has dissolved.

2. Whisk together the egg yolks and ½ cup (100g) sugar in a medium bowl until the mixture is light and fluffy.

3. Add the flour to the egg-yolk mixture, a little bit at a time, along with about ¼ cup (60ml) of the boiling cream and milk mixture, whisking them together to combine. Once all the flour is fully incorporated, pour this mixture into the saucepan with the remainder of the boiling milk/cream. Without taking the pan off the stove, carefully stir the mixture until it has thickened and boiled again, after about 30 seconds over high heat. Remove the pan from the heat. Allow the custard to cool before using.

Crema Chantilly

(CHANTILLY CREAM)

THIS IS A CLASSIC, SIMPLE RECIPE USED TO FILL CREAM PUFFS AND CAKES, OR TO LIGHTEN CUSTARDS.

PREP TIME: *10 minutes* | SERVES: *8*

INGREDIENTS

2 cups (500g) heavy whipping cream, chilled

¼ cup (50g) sugar

½ vanilla bean, seeds scraped out

INSTRUCTIONS

1. In a mixing bowl, using a handheld mixer or an electric stand mixer with a beater attachment, whip the chilled cream with the sugar and vanilla seeds until the mixture forms firm peaks. Use it right away or store it in the fridge for later use.

Crema Diplomatica

(DIPLOMAT CUSTARD)

THIS SOFT AND DELICATE CUSTARD, A COMBINATION OF VANILLA CUSTARD AND
CHANTILLY CREAM, IS USED TO MAKE A WIDE VARIETY OF PASTRIES AND CAKES,
AND IT'S ALSO ONE OF THE MOST DELICIOUS ELEMENTS OF MY FATHER IVAN'S
FAVORITE CAKE (PAN DI SPAGNA RUM E CREMA [RUM-SOAKED SPONGE CAKE WITH
CREAM AND FRUIT], PAGE 202). THE LIGHTNESS OF THIS CUSTARD PAIRS PERFECTLY
WITH EITHER FRESH FRUIT OR CHOCOLATE. FOR THIS RECIPE, MAKE SURE THAT ALL
THE COMPONENTS ARE COLD WHEN YOU COMBINE THE VANILLA CUSTARD WITH THE
CHANTILLY CREAM.

PREP TIME: *45 minutes* | SERVES: *8–10*

INGREDIENTS

Crema Pasticcera (Vanilla Custard)
(page 166)

Crema Chantilly (Chantilly Cream)
(page 168)

INSTRUCTIONS

1. Make a batch of Vanilla Custard (page 166).

2. Make a batch of Chantilly Cream (page 168).

3. Assembly: Combine the Vanilla Custard with the Chantilly Cream.

Crema al Cioccolato

(CHOCOLATE CUSTARD)

CHOCOLATE CUSTARD IS ONE OF THE MAIN PLAYERS IN THE WORLD OF PASTRY CREAM, AND ONE OF MY GREAT-AUNT MAGDA'S FAVORITES. ALTHOUGH SHE LIVED WITH MY FAMILY AND HELPED RAISE MY BROTHER AND ME, JUST AS MY MOM DID, WE ALWAYS SAW HER AS OUR GRANDMA. SHE USED TO MAKE *TORTA DEL NONNO* (GRANDFATHER'S PIE) (SEE PAGE 207), A CLASSIC CAKE FROM TUSCANY. IT WAS HER FAVORITE.

PREP TIME: *15 minutes* | COOKING TIME: *10 minutes*

INGREDIENTS

4 cups (950ml) milk

⅓ cup (80ml) heavy whipping cream

1 vanilla bean, seeds scraped out

1¼ cups (250g) sugar

10 egg yolks

½ cup (100g) sugar

½ cup (60g) all-purpose flour

1 pound, 3 ounces (19 ounces) (550g) dark chocolate (at least 70% cocoa), coarsely chopped

INSTRUCTIONS

1. Pour the milk and heavy whipping cream into a large saucepan. Add the vanilla bean seeds and 1¼ cups (250g) sugar and bring the mixture to a boil.

2. Meanwhile, whisk together the egg yolks and ½ cup (100g) sugar in a medium bowl until the mixture is light and fluffy.

3. Once the milk mixture has come to a boil, add the flour to the egg-yolk mixture, a little bit at a time, along with a small amount of the boiling milk. Once the flour is fully incorporated, pour this mixture into the boiling milk. Without taking the pan off the stove, carefully stir the cream until it is thick and boils again, making sure the custard at the bottom of the pan does not burn.

4. Take the saucepan off the stove. Stir the chocolate into the hot milk mixture and mix it well with a whisk until the chocolate has dissolved. Cool the chocolate and use it with your favorite pastry.

Torta della Nonna

(GRANDMA'S PIE)

THIS IS ONE OF THE EASIEST, BUT MOST AMAZING DESSERTS YOU WILL EVER MAKE. TO ME, IT REPRESENTS THE VERY BEST OF ITALIAN COOKING: THE PERFECT COMBINATION OF SIMPLE INGREDIENTS AND FARM-FRESH PRODUCTS.

PREP TIME: *30 minutes*　|　COOKING TIME: *30 minutes*　|　SERVES: *10*

INGREDIENTS

Pasta Frolla (Basic Shortbread) (see recipe on page 153)

Crema Pasticcera (Vanilla Custard) (see recipe on page 166)

FOR THE TOPPING

1–2 tablespoons pine nuts

1–2 tablespoons sliced almonds

Powdered sugar, as a garnish

INSTRUCTIONS

1. Make the *Pasta Frolla* shortbread dough.

2. Prepare the Vanilla Custard.

3. Preheat the oven to 350°F (180°C).

4. Assembly: Using a rolling pin, roll out one of the Pasta Frolla shortbread disks to form a thin circle about ⅛ inch (3mm) thick, and roughly 12 inches (30cm) in diameter. This is for the bottom crust. Roll out the other shortbread disk, about ⅛ inch (3mm) thick, to form a circle, roughly ½ inch (12mm) thick and 10 inches (25cm) in diameter, for the top crust. Make sure the pastry dough is cold, as that will make it much easier to form the crust.

5. Carefully line a 9-inch (23cm) aluminum tart pan with the round (bottom) shortbread crust.

6. Bake the shortbread crust for 10 minutes at 350°F (180°C).

7. When the crust is cool, spoon the cool Vanilla Custard (see recipe below) into a pastry bag fitted with a ½-inch (12mm) plain tip and pipe the custard into the crust, filling it completely. Set the tart pan aside while you make the lattice for the top of the pie.

8. Using a small knife, cut a few strips from the square piece of pastry and place them on top of the pie, spacing them ¼ inch (6mm) apart. Repeat this step in the opposite direction to create a beautiful lattice top for the pie.

9. Put the pie back into the oven and bake for 8 minutes or so (at 350°F [180°C]). Then sprinkle a handful of pine nuts and sliced almonds on top and continue to bake the pie for about 30 more minutes, or until the top is golden brown.

10. Once the pie is done, let it cool down a bit and then remove it from the tart pan. Transfer it to a large serving plate and sprinkle some powdered sugar on top. Enjoy the pie while it is still warm. Buon appetito!

Torta di Pere

(CHOCOLATE AND PEAR PIE)

THIS IS MY BROTHER MASSIMILIANO'S GREAT RECIPE. THE DELICACY OF THE PEARS, COMBINED WITH DARK CHOCOLATE AND THE BUTTERY, NUTTY FLAVOR OF ALMONDS, MAKES THIS PIE ONE OF THE BEST I'VE EVER EATEN. TRY IT AND SEE FOR YOURSELF. IT COMES TOGETHER QUICKLY IF YOU'VE PREPARED THE *PASTA FROLLA* (BASIC SHORTBREAD) FOR THE CRUST (PAGE 153) BEFOREHAND.

PREP TIME: *25 minutes* | COOKING TIME: *35 minutes* | SERVES: *8–10*

INGREDIENTS

Pasta Frolla (Basic Shortbread) (for the bottom of the pie) (page 153)

FOR THE FILLING

2 ½ ounces (70g) dark chocolate (at least 70% cocoa), broken into pieces.

5 cups (1L) milk

1 vanilla bean, seeds scraped out

3 pears, peeled and halved

FOR THE SBRISOLONA CRUNCHY TART CRUST (TOP OF THE PIE)

8 tablespoons (110g) unsalted butter, softened to room temperature

½ cup (100g) sugar

½ cup (60g) almond flour

½ cup (60g) all-purpose flour

Powdered sugar, to sprinkle on top

Cocoa powder, to sprinkle on top

INSTRUCTIONS

1. Preheat the oven to 350°C (180°C).

2. Make the *Pasta Frolla* (Basic Shortbread) (page 153), and roll it out into a circle, roughly ¼ inch (6mm) thick and 12 inches (30cm) in diameter. Lightly press the dough into the bottom of a 9-inch (23cm) tart pan. Bake the crust for no more than 10 minutes and then set it aside to cool on a wire rack.

3. To make the filling: In a heavy-bottomed saucepan, melt the dark chocolate. Once it is melted, pour the chocolate over the prepared bottom crust, spreading it evenly with a silicone (heat-resistant) spatula. (This chocolate layer will keep the crust from getting soggy when the pears are added to the tart shell.) Allow the chocolate to cool and harden.

4. Pour the milk into a saucepan and add the vanilla seeds and pears. Cook the pears for 5–10 minutes on medium heat until caramelized (they are soft). Remove the pears from the pan and transfer them to a cutting board. Discard the milk-and-vanilla mixture. When the pears are cool enough to handle, slice and layer them on top of the chocolate crust.

5. To make the sbrisolona, crunchy tart crust (top of the pie): In the bowl of an electric stand mixer, fitted with a paddle attachment, or using a handheld mixer, combine the butter, sugar, almond flour, and all-purpose flour, just until you get a crumblike mixture for the crumbly "topping." If you overmix the ingredients, you will make a cookie dough that will not have the consistency needed for the top crust.

6. Assembly: Preheat the oven to 350°F (180°C).

7. Scatter the crumbly sbrisolona crust mixture over the pears, covering them completely. Bake the pie for 25–30 minutes. Let the pie cool before removing it from the tart pan. Sprinkle powdered sugar and cocoa powder on top before serving.

Torta di Ricotta

(RICOTTA PIE)

THE SIMPLE, FRESH INGREDIENTS IN THIS TART-LIKE RICOTTA CHEESE AND LEMON ZEST-SUMMON THE BEST FLAVORS AND AROMAS OF THE MEDITERRANEAN AND SOUTHERN ITALY.

PREP TIME: *15 minutes* | COOKING TIME: *45 minutes* | SERVES: *8–10*

Pasta Frolla (Basic Shortbread)
(page 153)

2½ ounces (70g) dark chocolate
(64–70% cocoa), broken into pieces

3 cups (500g) ricotta cheese

4–5 eggs

1¼ cups (170g) powdered sugar, plus
more for sprinkling on top

Zest of 1 lemon

½ cup (120ml) heavy cream

INSTRUCTIONS

1. Preheat the oven to 350°C (180°C).

2. Prepare *Pasta Frolla* (Basic Shortbread, page 153) and divide the shortbread into 2 equal-sized disks of dough, which will become the crust. Roll each of the shortbread crusts into a circle roughly 12 inches (30cm) in diameter. Place 1 shortbread crust on the bottom of a 9-inch (23cm) round, 2-inch (5cm) high tart pan, and up the sides of the tart pan. Bake for 10 minutes and set aside.

3. In a heavy-bottomed saucepan, melt the dark chocolate. Once it is melted, pour the chocolate over the prepared bottom crust in the tart pan, spreading it evenly with a silicone (heat-resistant) spatula. Allow the chocolate to cool and harden.

4. Preheat the oven to 325°F (160°C).

5. In a mixing bowl, place the ricotta cheese, eggs, powdered sugar, and lemon zest. Combine thoroughly, until the mixture is smooth, and then add the heavy cream, mixing it in completely. Pour the mixture into the prepared tart pan, on top of the chocolate layer, leaving at least ½ inch (12mm) between the filling and the top of the crust; otherwise, it will spill over the sides of the pan while baking.

6. Bake the tart for at least 35 minutes or until it sets and the top starts to turn golden brown. If you notice any cracking in the crust, turn the temperature down to 300°F (150°C). Serve the tart at room temperature with a sprinkle of powdered sugar on top.

Torta Paradiso

(PARADISE PIE)

AFTER MUCH TESTING, THIS CAKE WAS DEVELOPED IN PAVIA, ITALY, IN 1878, IN THE PASTRY SHOP OF ENRICO VIGONI. LEGEND HAS IT THAT A LOCAL NOBLEWOMAN WHO TASTED THE SWEET PASTRY GAVE THE FOLLOWING VERDICT: "THIS CAKE IS PARADISE." IT SOON BECAME A SYMBOL OF PAVIA AND A CLASSIC OF ITALIAN PASTRY—A MIX OF SIMPLE INGREDIENTS THAT ARE REMINISCENT OF SPONGE CAKE, BUT, WITH THE ADDITION OF BUTTER AND BAKING POWDER, THE RESULT IS AN EXTREMELY LIGHTWEIGHT, LOFTY, HEAVENLY CAKE THAT IS AS SOFT AS A CLOUD.

PREP TIME: *20 minutes* | COOKING TIME: *30 minutes* | SERVES: *8–10*

INGREDIENTS

8 tablespoons (110g) unsalted butter, plus more for buttering the pan

¾ cup (100g) powdered sugar

1 vanilla bean, seeds scraped out

Zest of 1 lemon

Pinch of salt

1 whole egg

6 egg yolks

⅓ cup (50g) all-purpose flour

⅓ cup (50g) potato starch

1 teaspoon (2.5g) baking powder

INSTRUCTIONS

1. Preheat the oven to 350°F (180°C).

2. In the bowl of an electric stand mixer fitted with a whisk (or using a handheld mixer), beat the butter with the powdered sugar, vanilla seeds, lemon zest, and salt for about 5 minutes until creamy. Mix in the whole egg without slowing the mixing speed. Continue to mix, while incorporating all the egg yolks. Once this is done, you should have an airy, soft mixture.

3. In a separate bowl sift together the flour, potato starch, and baking powder. Slowly fold these dry ingredients into the mixing bowl with the butter-egg mixture, scraping from the bottom of the bowl to the top. Overmixing will result in a very dense pie.

4. Butter a 9-inch (23cm) pie pan and fill it ¾ full with the batter. Bake the pie for at least 30 minutes. Poke the middle of the pie with a toothpick, and if it comes out clean, the pie is done.

Torta di Verdure

THE CUISINE OF LUCCA, MY HOMETOWN, IS ONE OF THE TASTIEST IN TUSCANY. THE DELICIOUS TORDELLI, THE SOUPS, THE TRADITIONAL *BUCCELLATO*, AND MANY OTHER DELICACIES DELIGHT EVEN THE MOST DISCERNING PALATES. *TORTA DI VERDURE* IS A CROWN-SHAPED PASTRY SHELL FILLED WITH VEGETABLES AND SPICES THAT ADD UP TO A FASCINATING, BALANCED BLEND OF SWEET AND SALTY. A SWEET VEGETABLE PIE? YES, AND I ASSURE YOU IT IS EXQUISITE. MAKE IT AND SEE FOR YOURSELF!

PREP TIME: *30 minutes* | COOKING TIME: *40–45 minutes, until golden brown* | SERVES: *8–10*

FOR THE CRUST

12 tablespoons (170g) unsalted butter, cubed

¾ cup (90g) powdered sugar

2 egg yolks

2 cups (250g) all-purpose flour

Zest of ½ lemon

1 teaspoon (5ml) pure vanilla extract

FOR THE FILLING

½ cup (100g) Arborio rice

¾ cup (180ml) water

1 cup (240ml) milk, plus a bit more for soaking the bread crumbs

½ cup sugar plus 1 tablespoon (110g)

1 cup (125g) bread crumbs

4 tablespoons (60g) unsalted butter

1 bunch chard, leaves only, finely chopped

1 handful parsley, finely chopped

1 tablespoon (5g) parmigiano, grated

½ cup (60g) pine nuts

⅓ cup (50g) raisins

Pinch of cinnamon

Pinch of nutmeg

2 eggs

Pinch of salt

Pinch of pepper

INSTRUCTIONS

1. To make the crust: In the bowl of an electric stand mixer, fitted with a hook attachment, combine the butter and powdered sugar. Mix at the lowest speed. Once the butter and sugar are fully combined, add the egg yolks. Incorporate the flour all at once, mixing it in thoroughly. Add the lemon zest and vanilla to the dough and mix it in gently.

2. Turn the dough onto a floured work surface and knead it quickly. Flatten the dough into a disk and wrap it in wax paper. Refrigerate the dough for about 30 minutes to 1 hour (overnight, however, is preferable), then roll out the dough. When you have a round piece that measures roughly 12 inches (30cm) in diameter, place it in 9-inch (23cm) pie pan.

3. To make the filling: Put the rice, water, milk, and ½ cup (100g) sugar in a saucepan and cook covered over medium heat until the rice has absorbed all the liquid, about 30 minutes. Soak the bread crumbs in a little bit of milk, just enough to moisten them.

4. In a skillet, melt the butter and sauté the chard. Take the pan off the heat, and add the parsley and parmigiano.

5. Preheat the oven to 350°F (180°C).

6. Place the sautéed greens in a large bowl. Add the rice. Squeeze any excess milk out of the bread crumbs and add them to the bowl. Add the pine nuts, raisins, and cinnamon to the bowl, and mix to combine.

7. In a small bowl, combine the nutmeg, eggs, 1 tablespoon (10g) sugar, and salt and pepper. Mix well. Add this mixture to the bowl with the sautéed greens, rice, and bread crumbs, and mix well.

8. Spoon the mixture into the crust. With your thumb and forefinger, gently pull the dough and form it into small peaks, at intervals, to make the crust resemble a crown. Bake the pie for 25–30 minutes, or until the mixture is firm and the "crown" is golden.

Torta di Mele

(APPLE PIE)

APPLE PIE IS A CLASSIC DESSERT THAT IS BELOVED ALL OVER THE WORLD. OVER
TIME, IT HAS TAKEN ON THE SPECIAL CHARACTERISTICS OF THE PLACES IN WHICH IT
IS PREPARED. THE USE OF APPLES IN DESSERTS HAS SPREAD ALMOST EVERYWHERE,
SO YOU CAN FIND MOST OF THE INGREDIENTS IN AMERICAN APPLE PIE IN THE
NEAREST STRUDEL OR APPLE CAKE, LIKE THIS CLASSIC ITALIAN VERSION. IT IS
SIMPLE AND QUICK TO PREPARE, AND THE RESULT IS A DELIGHTFULLY SOFT AND
CREAMY CAKE.

PREP TIME: *20 minutes* | COOKING TIME: *60 minutes* | SERVES: *8*

INGREDIENTS

4–5 (700g) apples*

Juice of 1 lemon

2 eggs

1 cup (200g) sugar

8 tablespoons (110g) unsalted butter,
melted, plus more to grease the pan

Zest of 1 lemon

1 teaspoon (2.5g) cinnamon

1 cup (240ml) milk

1 teaspoon (2.5g) baking powder

1 vanilla bean, seeds scraped out

Pinch of salt

1¼ cups (150g) all-purpose flour, plus
more to flour the pan

Powdered sugar and cinnamon, for
sprinkling on top of the cake

INSTRUCTIONS

1. Preheat the oven to 350°F (180°C).

2. Peel and slice the apples. Place the slices in a container with a mixture of water
and lemon juice; this will prevent the apples from turning brown.

3. In a large bowl, use a whisk to mix the eggs with the sugar. When they are
completely combined, add the melted butter. Gradually mix in the lemon zest,
cinnamon, milk, baking powder, vanilla seeds, and salt. Add the flour to the bowl
and stir it in very well to get a smooth mixture that is not too liquidy. Remove the
apple slices from the lemon-and-water mixture and drain them well. Gently stir them
into the batter.

4. Butter and flour a 9-inch (23cm) cake pan and pour in the batter. Lightly sprinkle the surface with a mixture of powdered sugar and cinnamon. Bake the cake for 50–60 minutes, until it is golden brown.

5. Take the cake out of the oven, then out of the pan, and place it on a wire rack to cool slightly before serving. To serve, sprinkle the surface again with a mix of powdered sugar and cinnamon.

*NOTE: Typically, I use any one (or a combination) of these sweet apples in Torta di Mele: Golden Delicious, Fuji, and Royal Gala.

Pasticceria Mignon

(BITE-SIZED PASTRIES)

BITE-SIZED PASTRIES ARE BECOMING INCREASINGLY POPULAR, AND YOU'LL WANT TO MAKE A SELECTION OF THEM FOR YOUR NEXT PARTY. YOUR GUESTS WILL LOVE TO NOSH ON THESE SMALL BITES OF INDULGENCE, EACH WITH A UNIQUE FLAVOR AND PERSONALITY.

INGREDIENTS

Pâte à Choux (Basic Cream Puff Pastry) (page 158)

Zabaione Cream (recipe below)

INSTRUCTIONS

1. Make the *Pâte à Choux* (Basic Cream Puff Pastry) (page 158).

2. Now your cream puffs are ready to be filled with zabaione cream (see below).

Zabaione Cream

ZABAIONE CREAM IS ONE OF THE MOST POPULAR, CLASSIC RECIPES USED IN ITALIAN PASTRIES: IT IS A RICH MIX OF EGG YOLKS, SUGAR, AND A GENEROUS SPLASH OF SWEET MARSALA, WHICH IS THEN "COOKED" IN A HOT WATER BATH UNTIL IT BECOMES THICK, FROTHY, AND IRRESISTIBLY DELICIOUS.

PREP TIME: *15 minutes* | COOKING TIME: *25 minutes* | SERVES: *4*

8 eggs

¾ cup (175g) sugar

⅜ cup (90ml) sweet Marsala wine

INSTRUCTIONS

1. Separate the yolks from the eggs (reserve the whites for use another time). Place the yolks and the sugar in a heavy aluminum bowl. Beat the egg yolks and sugar with a whisk or an electric mixer until an airy, foamy, smooth, almost-white cream is formed. Gradually stir in the Marsala wine, always beating to absorb the liquid.

2. When all the ingredients are well blended, set the aluminum bowl over a large pot, filled ⅓ with hot water, over low heat. The water must be simmering, not boiling. Stir the mixture with a whisk for 10–15 minutes, until you see the cream thicken and become smooth. Remove the Zabaione Cream from the heat and set it aside to cool, continuing to mix it with a whisk until it has cooled down to room temperature; otherwise, the wine will separate from the mixture.

3. Spoon the zabaione cream into a pastry bag fitted with a ½-inch (12mm) plain tip. Poke a whole with the pastry tip into the bottom of each cream puff and fill it with the zabaione cream.

Bigné allo Zabaione

(ZABAIONE CREAM PUFFS)

THESE BITE-SIZED CREAM PUFFS (PÂTE À CHOUX), FILLED WITH ZABAIONE (A RICH, SWEET CREAM, SPIKED WITH MARSALA), ARE AN ITALIAN CLASSIC. AND FOR GOOD REASON: THEY ARE DELIGHTFULLY LIGHT, INTENSELY FLAVORFUL, AND LITERALLY MELT IN YOUR MOUTH.

PREP TIME: *30 minutes* | COOKING TIME: *15 minutes* | SERVES: *10–12 (Makes approximately 60 cream puffs)*

INGREDIENTS

Pâte à Choux (Basic Cream Puff Pastry) (page 158)

Zabaione Cream (page 184)

SUGAR ICING

1 cup (120g) confectioners' sugar

2–6 tablespoons (30ml–90ml) milk or other liquid

½ teaspoon vanilla extract

1–2 drops pink food coloring

INSTRUCTIONS

1. Make the *Pâte à Choux* (Basic Cream Puff Pastry) (page 158). Now your cream puffs are ready to be filled with Zabaione Cream.

2. To make the Zabaione Cream, see page 184. Spoon the Zabaione Cream into a pastry bag fitted with a ½ inch (12mm) plain tip. Poke a hole with the pastry tip into the bottom of each cream puff and fill it with the Zabaione Cream.

3. To make the sugar icing, combine the sugar in a bowl with 2 tablespoons of the milk and the vanilla extract. Stir into a smooth paste. Add more milk to thin the icing, if you prefer a glaze. Add 1–2 drops of pink food coloring to the icing.

4. To finish the cream puffs, cut a small hole in a pastry bag, spoon the icing into it, then pipe the icing onto the cream puffs.

Cannoli di Ricotta

(RICOTTA-FILLED CANNOLIS)

THIS IS A CLASSIC DESSERT BORN IN SICILY, A LARGE ISLAND (THE LARGEST IN THE MEDITERRANEAN SEA), LOCATED SOUTH OF THE ITALIAN PENINSULA. *CANNOLI DI RICOTTA* WERE ORIGINALLY MADE DURING THE REGION'S CARNIVAL, AND LATER BECAME AN EVERYDAY DESSERT THAT CONTINUES TO BE ENJOYED THROUGHOUT THE YEAR. CANNOLIS ARE WELL-KNOWN AND BELOVED FIXTURES IN PASTRY SHOPS ALL OVER THE WORLD. THIS RECIPE CALLS FOR CANNOLI MOLDS, SO IF YOU LOVE CANNOLIS, AND WANT TO MAKE THEM, YOU'LL NEED TO INVEST IN SOME METAL CANNOLI MOLDS TO MAKE THE SHELLS.

PREP TIME: *60 minutes* | COOKING TIME: *50 minutes* | MAKES: *24 cannoli*

FOR THE CANNOLI SHELLS

1½ cups (190g) all-purpose flour

Pinch of salt

Pinch of cinnamon

Pinch of instant coffee

1 teaspoon (2g) cocoa powder

1 teaspoon (2.5g) powdered sugar

1 teaspoon (5g) unsalted butter or lard

1 egg

1 teaspoon (5ml) white wine vinegar

1 teaspoon (5ml) dry Marsala wine

2 egg whites

Vegetable oil (enough to make 2–3 inches [5–8cm] in the frying pot)

FOR THE FILLING

1 cup (250g) ricotta cheese

¾ cup (150g) sugar

1 cup (240g) heavy cream

¼ cup (40g) mini dark chocolate chips

¼ cup (35g) candied orange

FOR THE GARNISH

Pistachio nuts, chopped

Chocolate chips

Powdered sugar

INSTRUCTIONS

1. Spoon the ricotta cheese into a colander, and place it over a bowl to drain. Put the bowl in the fridge.

2. To make the cannoli shells: In a large bowl, sift together the flour, salt, cinnamon, instant coffee, cocoa powder, and powdered sugar. Add the butter (or lard), and the egg and use a pastry cutter to combine the mixture until it is crumbly (the butter and egg yolks should be thoroughly mixed into the dry ingredients). In small bowl mix the vinegar with the Marsala wine and add it very slowly to the flour mixture. You may not need to use all the liquid, depending on how much the flour absorbs. The dough should be soft and flexible but firm, a bit tougher than bread dough.

3. Knead the mixture for 5 minutes on a work surface until it is elastic, smooth, and homogeneous. Form it into a ball and wrap it in plastic wrap. Let it rest for at least 1 hour in the fridge.

4. To make the ricotta filling: Place the well-drained ricotta cheese in a bowl and add the sugar. Mix to blend, without overmixing.

5. In a separate bowl, or in the bowl of an electric stand mixer, fitted with a whisk attachment, whip the cream until it forms stiff peaks. Gently fold the cream into the ricotta mixture and stir in the chocolate chips and bits of candied orange. Cover the bowl with plastic wrap and refrigerate for at least 1 hour.

6. To make and fry the cannoli shells: In a medium-size saucepan with a heavy bottom, heat the oil (or lard) to 350°F–375°F (180°C–190°C).

7. Meanwhile, on a floured work surface roll out the cannoli shell dough (or use a pasta machine) until it is very thin, about ⅛ inch (3mm) thick. Using round pastry rings (or a small water glass) with a diameter of 3–4 inches (8–10cm), cut out 24 circles. Using your hands, gently reshape the dough circles into ovals. Wrap each dough oval around a cannoli mold, taking care to brush the ends with egg white to help seal them. Gently press the dough around the molds to make sure the cannoli dough won't fall off the molds during frying.

8. To fry the dough, use tongs to hold the edge of each mold as you submerge it in the hot oil (or lard). Fry the shells for 2–3 minutes, or until they're crispy and golden brown. Place the cannolis in their molds on a pile of paper towels to drain and cool completely before removing the shells from the molds.

9. Filling and Assembly: Once the shells are cool, fill a pastry bag—with a plain, wide nozzle—with the ricotta-cheese mixture and pipe it into both ends of each cannoli shell. Garnish the cannolis with pistachio nuts on one end and chocolate chips on the other. To serve, sprinkle the cannolis with a little powdered sugar.

Crostatina di Frutta

MY FAVORITE DESSERT IS A FRESH TART THAT COMBINES FRUIT, CREAM, AND A LIGHT, BUTTERY CRUST. WHEN I WAS GROWING UP IN ITALY, THE FARM ACROSS THE STREET FROM MY HOUSE SUPPLIED US WITH JUST ABOUT ALL THE FRESH PRODUCE, MILK, AND EGGS WE NEEDED, INCLUDING THE FRUIT FOR THIS DELICIOUS, CREAMY TART, WHICH MY MOM MADE FOR ALMOST ALL OF MY BIRTHDAYS.

BEAR IN MIND THAT YOU'LL NEED TO PREPARE THE CREMA DIPLOMATICA (*DIPLOMAT CUSTARD*) (PAGE 169), A COMBINATION OF *CREMA PASTICCERA* (VANILLA CUSTARD) AND *CREMA CHANTILLY* (CHANTILLY CREAM), BEFORE YOU MAKE THE SHORTBREAD CRUST FOR THIS DELECTABLE TART.

PREP TIME: *50 minutes* | COOKING TIME: *20 minutes* | SERVES: *8–10*

Pasta Frolla (Basic Shortbread) (page 153)

2 cups (480g) *Crema Diplomatica* (Diplomat Custard) (page 169))

1 cup (120g) each fresh seasonal fruit (strawberries, blackberries blueberries, raspberries)

INSTRUCTIONS

1. Make the *Pasta Frolla* (Basic Shortbread) dough (page 153), and chill the dough for at least 30 minutes.

2. Preheat the oven to 350°F (180°C).

3. On a lightly floured surface, roll out the chilled shortbread dough with a rolling pin to a desired thickness of ¼ inch (6mm). Cut out 8–10 circles of dough 3 inches (8cm) in diameter and press them gently into mini tart molds, pressing the dough up the sides of the molds. Bake for 18 minutes, until they are golden brown. Cool the tartlets in their molds on a wire rack.

4. Once the tarts are cool, remove them from the molds.

5. Make the *Crema Diplomatica* (Diplomat Custard) (page 169).

6. Once the cream is ready, fill a pastry bag with a round tip, and pipe the cream into the tart shells. Top the tarts with fresh strawberries, blackberries, blueberries, raspberries, or any fresh fruit that is in season.

Occhio di Bue

(BULL'S-EYE SHORTBREAD COOKIES)

NAMED FOR THEIR BULL'S-EYE SHAPE, THESE COOKIES ARE DELICIOUS PASTRIES
WITH A SOFT JAM OR CREAM FILLING. THEY'RE SIMPLE TO PREPARE, BUT LOOK
IMPRESSIVE. THE COOKIES CAN BE MADE IN VARIOUS SHAPES—CIRCLES, FLOWERS,
HEARTS—IN SHORT, ANYTHING THAT CAN BE FILLED WITH JAM, CHOCOLATE, OR
CHOCOLATE HAZELNUT CREAM, WHICH IS PARTICULARLY POPULAR IN ITALY.

PREP TIME: *10 minutes* | COOKING TIME: *25 minutes* | SERVES: *4*

Pasta Frolla (Basic Shortbread)
(page 153)

Chocolate Hazelnut spread (any good-
quality brand will do), to fill cookies

Powdered sugar, for dusting
the cookies

INSTRUCTIONS

1. To make the cookies: Prepare the *Pasta Frolla* (Basic Shortbread) (page 153), chill it, and then roll it out, to a thickness of about ⅛ inch (3mm), between 2 sheets of wax paper. If the dough becomes too soft to roll out, rewrap it in plastic and chill it until it's firm.

2. Preheat the oven to 350°F (180°C).

3. Cut out as many cookies as possible from the dough with a large cookie cutter, roughly 1½ inches (4cm) in diameter and place the cookies on 2 large, ungreased baking sheets, arranging the cookies about 1 inch (3cm) apart.

4. Using a smaller ½-inch (12mm) diameter cookie cutter, cut out centers from half the cookies, reserving the dough centers and rerolling them, along with the rest of the dough.

5. Bake the cookies for about 15 minutes, switching the position of the baking sheets halfway through baking, until the edges are lightly golden.

6. Let the cookies cool down completely on a wire rack.

7. Filling and assembly: Fill a pastry bag with chocolate hazelnut spread.

8. Pipe some of the spread onto the flat side of each cookie, and then place a cookie with a hole in the middle on top, making a sandwich. (You may also use jam or chocolate, if you like.) Dust the cookie rings (the cookies with a hole in the middle) with powdered sugar.

Baci di Dama

(LADY'S KISSES—ALMOND COOKIES SANDWICHED WITH DARK CHOCOLATE)

THESE FRAGRANT COOKIES, SANDWICHED WITH DARK CHOCOLATE, LOOK LIKE TWO LIPS KISSING, AND PAIR PERFECTLY WITH A CUP OF CAPPUCCINO.

PREP TIME: *60 minutes* | COOKING TIME: *30 minutes* | SERVES: *8 (Makes approximately 16 cookie sandwiches)*

FOR THE COOKIES

8 tablespoons (110g) unsalted butter

⅔ cup (80g) all-purpose flour

½ cup (100g) sugar

¾ cup (90g) almond flour

FOR THE CHOCOLATE GANACHE

⅓ cup (80ml) heavy whipping cream

1½ tablespoons (20g) unsalted butter

Pinch of salt

2 ounces (65g) roughly chopped dark chocolate (at least 70% cocoa)

INSTRUCTIONS

1. To make the cookies: In a mixing bowl, combine the butter, all-purpose flour, sugar, and almond flour with a wooden spoon or your fingers until the mixture is completely combined. Refrigerate the dough for 30 minutes or so.

2. Preheat the oven to 350°F (180°C).

3. Once the dough is chilled, remove it from the fridge and form the dough into small round balls (about 1 inch [3cm] for small cookies, but they can be made larger if desired). Place them on parchment paper or a pan liner on an ungreased baking sheet. Bake the cookies until golden brown, about 20 minutes.

4. Let the cookies cool completely on a wire rack.

5. To make the chocolate ganache: In a small heavy saucepan, bring the whipping cream and butter almost to a boil over medium-high heat and add the salt. Add the chocolate to the pan and let it melt into the almost boiling cream-and-butter mixture.

6. Remove the chocolate mixture from the stove and let it cool for about 10 minutes. Then stir the mixture with a whisk until it is smooth and glossy.

7. Transfer the ganache to a pastry bag fitted with a star tip.

8. Filling and assembly: Pipe the chocolate ganache on the flat side of each cookie, and then place another cookie on top, making a sandwich.

Funghetti al Cioccolato

(CHOCOLATE MUSHROOMS)

I LIKE THESE COOKIES BECAUSE THEY REMIND ME OF MY GRANDPA ROMANO, WHO USED TO TAKE MY BROTHER AND ME ON MUSHROOM-FINDING EXPEDITIONS IN THE FOREST. WE FOUND ALL KINDS OF FRESH MUSHROOMS, INCLUDING PORCINI AND GALLETTI, BUT THE BEST PART WAS HANGING OUT WITH GRANDPA. EVERY TIME I MAKE THESE DELICIOUS, MUSHROOM-SHAPED COOKIES, I THINK OF HIM.

PREP TIME: *45 minutes* | COOKING TIME: *45 minutes* | SERVES: *10–12*

Pâte à Choux (Basic Cream Puff Pastry) (page 158)

½ cup (150g) *Crema al Cioccolato* (Chocolate Custard) (page 000)

¼ cup (40g) whipped cream

FOR THE GARNISH

Powdered sugar

Cocoa powder

INSTRUCTIONS

1. Make the Pâte à Choux (Basic Cream Puff Pastry) (page 158).

2. Preheat the oven to 350°F (180°C).

3. Spoon the choux paste into a pastry bag and pipe out small cream puffs for the mushroom caps and small éclair shapes for the mushroom stems. Bake for about 20 minutes, until the mushroom caps and stems are golden brown around the edges.

4. While the mushroom puffs are baking, prepare the chocolate cream and chocolate custard.

5. Assembly: Once the Crema al Cioccolato (Chocolate Custard) is cold, combine it with the whipped cream and pipe the mixture into both the cream puff and the éclair underneath.

6. Then put the stem inside the cream puff so it will resemble a little mushroom.

7. Dust with powdered sugar and cocoa powder.

8. Serve fresh or keep in the fridge for 3–4 days at the most.

Tiramisù

MY MOM, LAURA, LOVES COFFEE AND CHOCOLATE. THIS RECIPE FOR TIRAMISÙ HAS
BEEN IN MY FAMILY FROM BEFORE I WAS BORN. THE CREAMINESS OF THE CAKE, WITH
ITS PURE, STRONG COFFEE TASTE, MAKES TIRAMISÙ ONE OF THE MOST POPULAR
CAKES EVER CREATED IN ITALY. THIS RECIPE GIVES YOU THE OPTION OF MAKING ONE
LARGE *GENOISE* SPONGE CAKE TO USE IN THE TIRAMISÙ OR YOU CAN PIPE *GENOISE*
(BASIC SPONGE CAKE) BATTER TO MAKE LADY FINGERS. EITHER WAY, THE RESULT
IS A WONDERFULLY DECADENT DESSERT.

PREP TIME: *40 minutes* | COOKING TIME: *5 minutes* | SERVES: *8*

FOR THE FILLING

6 eggs, separated

½ cup + 2 tablespoons (120g) sugar,
divided

2 cups (300g) mascarpone

3½ ounces (100g) dark chocolate (at
least 70% cocoa)

Genoise (Basic Sponge Cake) (page
154)

FOR SOAKING THE CAKE

Espresso coffee

Sugar, to taste

Cocoa powder, for sprinkling

INSTRUCTIONS

1. To make the filling: Whip the egg yolks with half the sugar until smooth and
creamy.

2. In a separate bowl, using a whisk or a handheld electric mixer, whip the
egg whites with the other half of the sugar until stiff peaks form, approximately
5 minutes.

3. In the bowl of an electric stand mixer, fitted with a whisk attachment (or using a
handheld mixer), whip the mascarpone and slowly incorporate the egg-yolk mixture.
By hand, gently fold in the egg whites.

4. Chop the dark chocolate and add it to the mascarpone mixture. Cover it with
plastic wrap and let it cool in the fridge for at least 30 minutes.

5. Make the Genoise (Basic Sponge Cake) (page 154).

6. When the cake is done (it will turn golden brown) remove it from the pan immediately and transfer it to a cooling rack.

7. When the cake is cool, cut it into 3 layers.

8. Assembly: Brew the coffee and add a little bit of sugar to taste.

9. Use a soaking bottle or pastry brush to soak the *Genoise* with the sweetened coffee.

10. Place the first layer of coffee-soaked *Genoise* in the bottom of a glass dish and pour over some of the tiramisù mixture. Repeat layering with the *Genoise* and tiramisù mixture 2 more times. To finish, top with a sprinkling of cocoa powder.

11. Cover with plastic wrap and refrigerate for at least 30 minutes before serving.

THE ORIGINS OF TIRAMISÙ

There are many stories about the origin of tiramisù. For example, according to one legend, dating back to the 1600s, a group of pastry chefs in Siena, Tuscany, decided to make a cake for the Grand Duke Cosimo III de' Medici. The chefs wanted it to reflect the qualities of the Grand Duke, so they needed to make an important, delicious dessert, made with simple ingredients. That tiramisù was called the "Soup of the Duke." Noble people at the time liked the dessert and thought it had aphrodisiac qualities.

Pan di Spagna Rum e Crema

(RUM-SOAKED SPONGE CAKE WITH CREAM AND FRUIT)

THIS IS MY FATHER IVAN'S FAVORITE DESSERT. HIS BIRTHDAY CAKE ALWAYS HAS TO HAVE FRESH CREAM, SOME GOOD OLD RUM, FRUIT–AND CHOCOLATE. MY DAD IS MY BIGGEST INSPIRATION AND THE PERSON WHO ALWAYS TAUGHT ME TO TRY AS HARD AS POSSIBLE, NEVER TO STOP, AND IF I MAKE A MISTAKE, PUT MY HEAD DOWN AND START AGAIN. PERSEVERANCE IS THE KEY TO SUCCESS!

THIS RECIPE TAKES A LITTLE PLANNING. START BY MAKING A PERFECT SPONGE CAKE (IT'S EASY) AND LET IT COOL DOWN. THEN MAKE THE *CREMA DIPLOMATICA* (DIPLOMAT CUSTARD) (PAGE 169), A COMBINATION OF *CREMA PASTICCERA* (VANILLA CUSTARD) AND *CREMA CHANTILLY* (CHANTILLY CREAM). AFTER THAT, IT'S ALL FUN– JUST ADD THE CUSTARD, CHOCOLATE, AND FRESH MIXED BERRIES–AND YOU HAVE A SUBLIMELY DECADENT DESSERT.

PREP TIME: *40 minutes* | COOKING TIME: *55 minutes* | SERVES: *8–10*

Pan di Spagna (Sponge Cake) (page 150)

2¼ cups (530ml) water

1 cup (250g) sugar

3¼ cups (750ml) rum

Crema Diplomatica (Diplomat Custard) (page 169)

6 strawberries, thinly sliced, plus more for garnish

1 cup (125g) raspberries

1 cup (125g) blueberries

1 cup (125g) strawberries

4 ounces (110g) white chocolate, roughly chopped

Edible flowers (optional)

INSTRUCTIONS

1. Preheat the oven to 350°F (180°C). Make the *Pan di Spagna* (Sponge Cake) (page 150). Let it cool on a wire rack.

2. Assembly: Bring the water and sugar to a boil in a saucepan. Let the mixture cool, and then add the rum. Place a baking sheet in the freezer to chill.

3. Cut the sponge cake in half horizontally. Brush the bottom half of the cake with the rum mixture, using a pastry brush.

4. Make the *Crema Diplomatica* (Diplomat Custard) (page 169). Using a pastry bag with a ½ inch (12mm) nozzle, pipe the Diplomat Custard over the surface, covering it up to ¼ inch (6mm) from the edges. Then scatter the sliced strawberries, half of the raspberries, and half of the blueberries over the Diplomat Custard. Place the other half of the cake on top of the fruit/cream layer. Pipe the top of the cake with an even layer of the Diplomat Custard and smooth it out with a small offset spatula.

5. Microwave the white chocolate at 15- to 20-second intervals, stirring between each interval, until the chocolate is almost completely melted. Remove it from the microwave when you can still see pieces of the chocolate. Continue to stir until the chocolate is completely smooth.

6. Remove the baking sheet from the freezer, and pour 2 thin strips of chocolate, each about ¹⁄₁₆ inch (1mm) thick, 3 inches (8cm) wide, and 15 inches (38cm) long (they can be slightly tapered at either end) onto the cold baking sheet. Put the baking sheet back in the freezer for just 1 or 2 minutes, until the white chocolate is set but still pliable. Once the chocolate is set, start at one end of a strip and use the edge of an offset spatula to lift and ease it off the baking sheet in one piece. Wrap the chocolate strip around the cake. Repeat with the second strip so that the ends overlap.

7. Cut the additional strawberries in half. Garnish the top of the cake with the remaining raspberries and blueberries, the halved strawberries, and edible flowers, if using.

Torta Rosita

(ROSITA'S PIE)

MY LITTLE GRANDMA ROSITA IS THE KINDEST PERSON I KNOW. SHE LOVES LIFE—AND SHE LOVES TO MAKE THIS PIE. WHEN I WAS A KID, SHE PREPARED IT WITHOUT THE ALCOHOL, BUT ONCE I GREW UP, I FINALLY GOT TO TRY THE REAL *TORTA ROSITA:* CHOCOLATE, CREAM, AND LIQUEUR IN BEAUTIFUL HARMONY!

ROSITA'S PIE HAS SEVERAL COMPONENTS, WHICH REQUIRE A LITTLE PLANNING. BEFORE YOU BAKE THE CAKE, PREPARE THE *CREMA AL CIOCCOLATO* (CHOCOLATE CUSTARD) (PAGE 170) AND *CREMA PASTICCERA* (VANILLA CUSTARD) (PAGE 166). AFTER THAT, IT'S A PIECE OF PIE.

PREP TIME: *40 minutes* | COOKING TIME: *10 minutes* | SERVES: *8–10*

FOR THE SPONGE CAKE

Pan di Spagna (Sponge Cake) (page 150)

FOR THE ALKERMES SOLUTION

7 tablespoons (100ml) water

5 tablespoons (60g) sugar

⅓ cup (240ml) Alkermes liqueur

1 cup (300g) *Crema al Cioccolato* (Chocolate Custard) (page 170)

1 cup (300g) *Crema Pasticcera* (Vanilla Custard) (page 166)

1 batch *Crema Chantilly* (Chantilly Cream) (page 168)

2½ ounces dark chocolate (at least 70% cocoa), finely chopped for garnish

INSTRUCTIONS

1. Make the *Pan di Spagna* (Sponge Cake) (page 202). Once the sponge cake is done, remove it from the oven and let it cool on a wire rack.

2. To make the Alkermes solution: Bring the water and sugar to a boil. Take it off the heat and allow it to cool. Add the Alkermes liqueur.

3. Assembly: Cut the sponge cake into horizontal pieces and soak it with the Alkermes solution using a soaking bottle or a pastry brush to soak.

4. Next, prepare the *Crema al Cioccolato* (Chocolate Custard) (page 170) and the *Crema Pasticerra* (Vanilla Custard) (page 166). (You can also prepare the custards ahead of time.)

5. Place the first layer of Alkermes-soaked sponge cake in the bottom of a large glass dish. Using a pastry bag, pipe the Chocolate Custard and Vanilla Custard, lightened with whipped cream, over the first layer to cover it. Place a layer of sponge cake over the Vanilla Custard and pipe Chocolate Custard over that layer. Repeat this layering process a couple of times.

6. Finish with a sprinkle of finely chopped dark chocolate on top.

Torta del Nonno

(GRANDFATHER'S PIE)

THIS IS MY GRANDPA'S FAVORITE PIE, AS ITS ITALIAN NAME SUGGESTS (*NONNO* IS "GRANDFATHER" IN ITALIAN). ENJOYING THIS PIE, WARM OUT OF THE OVEN, WITH A CUP OF COFFEE AND THE NEWSPAPER, IS HOW MY GRANDPA ALWAYS LIKED TO START HIS DAY.

PREP TIME: *30 minutes* | COOKING TIME: *15 minutes* | SERVES: *10*

FOR THE PIE

Pasta Frolla (Basic Shortbread) (page 153)

Crema al Cioccolato (Chocolate Custard) (page 170)

FOR THE TOPPING

Handful slivered almonds

Handful dark chocolate chips (70% cocoa)

Powdered sugar

Cocoa powder

INSTRUCTIONS

1. Make the *Pasta Frolla* (Basic Shortbread) (page 153) and refrigerate it in wax paper. Let it cool in the refrigerator.

2. Prepare the *Crema al Cioccolato* (Chocolate Custard) (page 170) and refrigerate until it is thoroughly chilled.

3. On a lightly floured work surface, using a rolling pin, roll out the shortbread into a thin (about ⅛ inch [3mm]) round shape, about 12 inches (30cm) in diameter. Reserve some of the dough to make the lattice—the dough strips—for the top of the tart. Make sure the shortbread dough is cold, which will make it easier to roll out.

4. Carefully line a 9-inch (23cm) pie pan with the shortbread round. Use a pastry bag to pipe the chocolate custard into the pie crust. Fill it completely.

5. Make the lattice for the top of the tart: Roll out the reserved dough into a 10 × 10-inch (25cm x 25cm) square, about ⅛ inch (3mm) thick. Using a paring knife, cut small strips of dough and put them on top of the pie, spacing them ¼ inch (6mm) apart. Repeat this step in the opposite direction to create a beautiful lattice for the top of the tart.

6. Put the pie pan in the oven; the pan should be directly on the oven rack to make sure the bottom of the tart will be fully cooked. After 7–8 minutes, scatter a handful of slivered almonds and chocolate chips on top of the tart. Bake the pie until the top is golden brown. If the pie is baking too fast (that is, it's browning on the edges but not fully cooked on the inside), decrease the temperature to 325°F (160°C).

7. When it's done, let the tart cool down a bit and remove it from the pan. Sprinkle some powdered sugar and cocoa powder on top and enjoy while it is still warm. *Buon appetito!*

Panna Cotta

(COOKED CREAM)

***PANNA COTTA* IS A VERY DELICATE DESSERT THAT ORIGINATED IN NORTHERN ITALY. IT IS APPRECIATED EVERYWHERE IN THE WORLD FOR ITS SIMPLICITY, EXQUISITE TEXTURE, AND THE SEEMINGLY ENDLESS VARIATIONS THAT CAN TRANSFORM IT INTO SOMETHING UNIQUE EVERY TIME IT IS PREPARED, WHETHER IT IS TOPPED WITH FRESH, SEASONAL FRUIT, CHOCOLATE SHAVINGS, OR EVEN A REDUCTION OF BALSAMIC VINEGAR!**

PREP TIME: *5 minutes* | SERVINGS: *4*

INGREDIENTS

3 sheets of gelatin (bronze) (available online) or 1 envelope (6g) of unflavored gelatin

2 tablespoons (30ml) cold water

2 cups (480g) heavy cream

½ cup (100g) sugar

½ vanilla bean, seeds scraped out

Zest of 1 orange

Pinch of salt

Fresh, seasonal berries, as garnish

INSTRUCTIONS

1. In a very small bowl, break the gelatin sheets into small pieces and submerge them in the cold water until the gelatin absorbs all the water.

2. In a large saucepan, combine the cream with the sugar, vanilla seeds, orange zest, and salt and bring to a boil. Remove the pan from the heat and stir in the gelatin.

3. Strain the cream mixture into a bowl and divide it among four ½ cup (120ml) ramekins and let it cool to room temperature. Cover the ramekins with plastic wrap and refrigerate them for at least 3 hours.

4. Serve the panna cotta cold, straight from the fridge, with freshly sliced strawberries or mixed berries on top.

Crème Brûlée

(CARAMELIZED CREAM)

THE ORIGIN OF *CRÊME BRÛLÉE*, FRENCH FOR "BURNED CREAM," GOES BACK TO THE LATE SEVENTEENTH CENTURY, WHEN IT WAS FORMALIZED AS A SIMPLE, BUT DIVINE RECIPE THAT COMBINES CREAM, EGG YOLKS, VANILLA, AND SUGAR. THE "BURNED" (CARAMELIZED) TOP NOT ONLY GIVES THE DESSERT ITS NAME, IT ACCOUNTS FOR ITS POPULARITY.

PREP TIME: *10 minutes* | COOKING TIME: *30 minutes* | SERVES: *4*

INGREDIENTS

2 cups (480g) heavy cream

½ vanilla bean, seeds scraped out

6 egg yolks

½ cup (100g) granulated sugar

Pinch of salt

Light brown sugar to caramelize on top

INSTRUCTIONS

1. Preheat the oven to 350°F (180°C).

2. In a small saucepan over medium-high heat, bring the cream and the vanilla bean seeds almost to a boil. In a bowl, whisk together the egg yolks, sugar, and salt. Once the cream almost comes to a boil, add the whisked egg yolks, sugar, and salt, and mix everything together well.

3. Pour the cream mixture into four ½-cup (120ml) ramekins. Put the ramekins into a large roasting pan filled with boiling water, about halfway up the sides of the ramekins. Then put the pan into the oven. Bake for about 20–30 minutes, or until the cream mixture starts to set. Remove the ramekins from the oven.

4. Allow the cream to cool. Before serving, sprinkle some brown sugar (about a tablespoon [10g]) on top of each ramekin and flambé the sugar with a kitchen torch, passing the flame in a circular motion a couple of inches (cm) over the top of each ramekin until the sugar turns golden brown and caramelizes into a smooth, hard disk. Serve the *crème brûlée* right away.

Profiteroles

THE *PROFITEROLE* IS A CLASSIC FRENCH PASTRY COMPOSED OF A CREAM PUFF COATED WITH A CHOCOLATE GLAZE AND FILLED WITH CREAM. IN MY HOMETOWN OF LUCCA, THE LOCAL BAKERY MAKES *PROFITEROLES* WITH ZABAIONE CREAM, WHICH MAKES THEM PARTICULARLY RICH AND DECADENT.

PREP TIME: *20 minutes* | COOKING TIME: *40 minutes* | MAKES: *About 16 cream puffs*

FOR THE CHOCOLATE GLAZE

1¼ cups (300ml) heavy cream

¼ cup (60ml) glucose syrup (available online)

10½ ounces (300g) dark chocolate, melted

4 tablespoons (60g) butter

FOR THE PROFITEROLES

Pate à Choux (Basic Cream Puff Pastry) (page 158)

Zabaione Cream (page 184)

INSTRUCTIONS

1. To make the chocolate glaze: In a small saucepan, bring the heavy cream to a boil. Once the cream is boiling, add the glucose syrup and let it dissolve, then add the melted dark chocolate and the butter. Stir to thoroughly combine the mixture. Remove the pan from the heat, covering it to keep the glaze warm enough to spoon over the filled *profiteroles*.

2. To make the *profiteroles*: Make the *Pate à Choux* (Basic Cream Puff Pastry) dough (page 158). Bake the cream puffs at 350°F (180°C) for about 20 minutes, or until they are golden.

3. When they're done, cut each profiterole in half crosswise. Poke the bottom of each cream puff with a pastry bag tip, fill it with the Zabaione Cream (page 184), and then drizzle the chocolate glaze over the top.

4. To serve, place 4 cream puffs on each plate.

L'ARTE DEL GELATO
(THE ART OF GELATO)

THIS BOOK WOULD BE INCOMPLETE WITHOUT A CHAPTER ON HOW TO MAKE FRESH, HOMEMADE GELATO. IN ITALY, OUR TAKE ON ICE CREAM—GELATO—IS DENSER, LESS AIRY, AND LESS FATTY THAN ICE CREAM IN THE UNITED STATES, AND, BECAUSE IT IS SERVED AT A SLIGHTLY WARMER TEMPERATURE THAN AMERICAN ICE CREAM, IT IS SUPER-SMOOTH. IT IS ALSO THE PERFECT MEDIUM TO SHOWCASE DELICIOUS, SWEET, SEASONAL FRUITS, SUCH AS STRAWBERRIES. GELATO IS AN IMPORTANT PART OF ITALIAN CULTURE AND LIFESTYLE, AND, OF COURSE, IT'S THE BEST WAY TO REFRESH THE SENSES WITH SOMETHING WONDERFULLY SWEET AND CREAMY.

FIOR DI LATTE *218*

(Milk-based Gelato)

CIOCCOLATO *220*

(Chocolate Gelato)

LIMONE *222*

(Lemon Gelato, Dairy-Free)

CREMA *224*

(Vanilla Custard Gelato)

FRAGOLA *225*

(Strawberry Gelato)

PISTACCHIO *226*

(Pistachio Gelato)

STRACCIATELLA *228*

(Chocolate Chip Gelato)

FRUTTI DI BOSCO SORBETTO *229*

(Wild Berry Sorbet)

ZUPPA INGLESE *230*

(Liqueur-Infused Sponge Cake with Custard Gelato)

Fior di Latte

(MILK-BASED GELATO)

VANILLA MILK IS THE SIMPLEST GELATO, AND THE MOST VERSATILE. IT CAN BE USED AS THE BASE FOR COUNTLESS ICE CREAM FLAVORS, OR, SIMPLY, AS A DELIGHTFUL TOPPING FOR A SLICE OF YOUR FAVORITE PIE.

PREP TIME: *20 minutes* | FREEZING TIME: *3–5 hours* | SERVES: *4–6*

INGREDIENTS

2½ cups (600 ml) milk

⅓ cup (80ml) heavy whipping cream

2 tablespoons (20g) dextrose

2 tablespoons (15g) powdered milk

1 egg yolk

¼ cup + 2 tablespoons (90g) sugar

1 vanilla bean, seeds scraped out

INSTRUCTIONS

1. In a small saucepan on the stove, place the milk, whipping cream, dextrose, powdered milk, egg yolk, and sugar. Stir to mix all the ingredients. Bring the mixture to a temperature of 180°F (85°C), stirring constantly.

2. Once the temperature of the mixture has reached 180°F (85°C) (you can verify the temperature using a probe), turn the heat off and transfer the mixture to a heatproof bowl. Incorporate the vanilla bean seeds, mixing them in well, and put the bowl in the refrigerator to cool. Once the gelato is chilled, whisk it to remove any lumps, and then put the bowl in the freezer. Mix the gelato every 30 minutes or so, over the course of 3–5 hours, in order to make it smooth and creamy. Alternatively, pour the mixture into an ice cream maker, and freeze according to the manufacturer's instructions.

Cioccolato

(CHOCOLATE GELATO)

THIS GELATO IS RICH, DARK, AND EXTRAORDINARILY CREAMY—EXACTLY WHAT I LIKE TO THINK OF AS THE PERFECT CHOCOLATE GELATO.

PREP TIME: *20 minutes* | FREEZING TIME: *3–5 hours* | SERVES: *4–6*

INGREDIENTS

¾ cup (175g) sugar

6 egg yokes

2½ cups (600ml) milk

⅔ cup (160ml) heavy whipping cream

1 teaspoon (5ml) liquid glucose (can be found online)

⅓ cup (50g) cocoa powder

INSTRUCTIONS

1. In a bowl, combine the sugar and egg yolks. Using an electric mixer, beat the yolks and sugar until the mixture thickens and turns pale. Set the mixture aside.

2. Place the milk, cream, and glucose in a heavy saucepan over medium heat for 5 minutes, and then add it to the bowl with the eggs and sugar. Stir the mixture with a whisk until all the ingredients are well combined. Pour this mixture into the saucepan over medium heat, stirring constantly, until it reaches a temperature of 180°F (85°C), (check the temperature with a probe). Do not bring the mixture to a boil or the yolks will form lumps.

3. Remove the saucepan from the heat and add the cocoa powder, stirring well.

4. Fill a large metal bowl halfway up with ice water.

5. Let the mixture cool down immediately by placing the saucepan in the bowl of ice water. Cover the gelato and refrigerate it for about 1 hour. Once the gelato is cold, whisk it to remove any lumps, and put it in the freezer. Whisk it again every 30 minutes, over the next 3–5 hours, to remove any lumps and create a smooth, creamy consistency. Alternatively, pour the mixture into an ice cream maker, and freeze according to the manufacturer's instructions.

Limone

THROUGHOUT MY CHILDHOOD, THE PERFUME OF LEMONS WAS A CONSTANT AND
FAMILIAR PRESENCE. TO ME, THIS WATER-BASED, DAIRY-FREE GELATO IS THE MOST
REFRESHING OF ALL, THANKS TO THE JUICE AND ZEST OF FRESH LEMONS.

PREP TIME: *20 minutes* | FREEZING TIME: *4 hours* | SERVES: *4–6*

1⅓ cups (315ml) water	Juice of 4 lemons
1 cup (200g) sugar	2 egg whites
Zest of 2 lemons	

INSTRUCTIONS

1. Pour the water and sugar into a small, heavy saucepan and bring the mixture to a boil, constantly stirring it, until the sugar has completely dissolved. Add the lemon zest to the saucepan and let it sit for at least 2 minutes, and then remove the pan from the heat. Transfer the mixture to a heatproof bowl and let it cool down in the fridge for 15–20 minutes.

2. Add the lemon juice to the chilled mixture. Use a sieve to strain it, and then whisk the mixture until it is smooth. In a separate bowl, beat the egg whites until they are foamy. Add the egg whites to the gelato and mix well. Cover the bowl and put it back in the freezer for about 4 hours, mixing it every 30 minutes or so to remove any lumps and create a silky, smooth consistency.

Crema

(VANILLA CUSTARD GELATO)

MY FAMILY AND I SPENT MANY SUMMERS IN PIANACCIO, A TOWN IN THE MOUNTAINS NEAR BOLOGNA, ITALY. WE USED TO GO TO A SMALL RESTAURANT THERE, AND GIANNI, THE OWNER, HAD AN ANTIQUE ICE CREAM MACHINE. HE MADE THE BEST FROZEN CUSTARD I'VE EVER HAD. RIGHT BEFORE HE PASSED, HE KINDLY SHARED THIS RECIPE WITH US.

PREP TIME: *25 minutes* | FREEZING TIME: *3–5 hours* | SERVES: *4–6*

2½ cups (600ml) milk

⅓ cup (80ml) heavy whipping cream

¼ cup + 2 tablespoons (90g) sugar

2 tablespoons (20g) dextrose

2 tablespoons (20g) powdered milk

5 egg yolks

1 vanilla bean, seeds scraped out

INSTRUCTIONS

1. Pour the milk into a small, heavy saucepan and add the whipping cream, sugar, dextrose, and powdered milk. Mix and add the egg yolks. Beat the mixture with a whisk until it is thick and smooth.

2. Add the vanilla bean seeds to the pan, stirring constantly, and bring the mixture to 180°F (85°C) (not a degree more, or the eggs will coagulate; you can use a probe to determine the temperature).

3. Fill a large metal bowl halfway up with ice water.

4. Turn off the heat, remove the pan, and place it in the metal bowl halfway filled with ice water. This will lower the temperature of the mixture. Keep stirring, for a few minutes, while the mixture cools. When it is cold, cover and refrigerate the mixture for at least 2 hours. Once it is chilled, put the gelato in the freezer and whisk it every 30 minutes, over the next 3–5 hours, to remove any lumps and create a smooth, creamy consistency. Alternatively, pour the mixture into an ice cream maker, and freeze according to the manufacturer's instructions.

Fragola

(STRAWBERRY GELATO)

MY UNCLE VINCENZO GREW STRAWBERRIES, AND I GREW UP HELPING HIM PLANT AND COVER THEM FOR THE HARD ITALIAN WINTERS. JUICY, SWEET STRAWBERRIES ALWAYS MADE THE PERFECT BASE FOR OUR FRUIT SALADS. HERE THEY ARE FEATURED IN A WINNING GELATO.

PREP TIME: *20 minutes* | FREEZING TIME: *3–5 hours* | SERVES: *4–6*

1⅓ cups (315ml) water

¾ cup (175g) sugar

About 20 fresh strawberries

2 egg whites, pasteurized

INSTRUCTIONS

1. Pour the water and sugar into a small, heavy saucepan and bring the mixture to a boil, constantly stirring it, until the sugar has completely dissolved.

2. Purée the strawberries in a blender and pour the strawberry purée into the saucepan with the water and sugar. Continue to boil the mixture for at least 2 minutes and then remove it from the heat. Let the strawberry mixture cool down and then put it in the fridge to chill for at least 4 hours or overnight (you want the strawberry flavor to intensify). Alternatively, pour the mixture into an ice cream maker, and freeze according to the manufacturer's instructions.

3. Transfer the strawberry mixture to another container and mix it, using a whisk, until it is smooth. In another bowl, beat the egg whites until they are foamy. Combine the egg whites with the strawberry mixture and mix well. Put the container in the freezer for about 3–5 hours, mixing it every 30 minutes or so to remove any lumps and create a smooth consistency.

Pistacchio

(PISTACHIO GELATO)

PISTACHIOS CULTIVATED IN THE BRONTE AREA OF SICILY ARE KNOWN AS "GREEN GOLD," BECAUSE THEY ARE SUCH AN IMPORTANT ECONOMIC RESOURCE FOR THE COMMUNITY. THE PISTACHIOS IN THIS CREAMY GELATO COMPLEMENT THE DELICATE SWEETNESS OF MILK TO SHOWCASE THEIR UNIQUE FLAVOR.

PREP TIME: *20 minutes* | FREEZING TIME: *3–5 hours* | SERVES: *4–6*

1 cup (120g) unsalted pistachios, plus more for garnish

1¼ cups (300ml) milk

⅔ cup (160ml) heavy whipping cream

2 tablespoons (20g) dextrose

2 tablespoons (20g) powdered milk

½ cup (100g), sugar, divided

1 egg yolk

INSTRUCTIONS

1. To toast the pistachios, spread them in a single layer on a baking sheet and bake them for 5–10 minutes at 350°F (180°C) until they're fragrant and light brown. When they are cool enough to handle, set aside a handful for garnish, then remove the shells and finely grind the nuts in a food processor until they become a paste.

2. Combine the milk, cream, dextrose, powdered milk, and a little more than ¼ cup (50g) of the sugar in a small, heavy saucepan. Stir the mixture well and bring it almost to a boil.

3. While the milk mixture is heating, beat the egg yolk with the remaining sugar in a medium bowl. Pour the hot milk mixture into the egg yolk, while stirring with a whisk. Transfer the mixture to a medium-size, heavy saucepan and heat it to 185°F (85°C), stirring constantly. Check the temperature of the mixture with a probe. Immediately transfer it to a heatproof bowl and add the pistachio paste. Combine the ingredients thoroughly with an immersion blender.

4. Fill a large metal bowl halfway up with ice water.

5. Let the mixture cool down immediately by placing it in the bowl of ice water. Cover the gelato and refrigerate it for about 1 hour. Once the mixture is chilled, whisk it to remove any lumps, and put it in the freezer. Whisk it again every 30 minutes, over the next 3–5 hours, to remove any lumps and make a creamy gelato. Alternatively, pour the mixture into an ice cream maker, and freeze according to the manufacturer's instructions. Garnish with toasted pistachios.

Stracciatella

(CHOCOLATE CHIP GELATO)

WHEN I WAS GROWING UP, I ATE THIS GELATO WITH MY FATHER ALL THE TIME, BECAUSE IT IS OUR FAVORITE. TRY IT AND SEE IF IT BECOMES YOUR FAVORITE, TOO.

PREP TIME: *20 minutes* | FREEZING TIME: *3–5 hours* | SERVES: *4–6*

2½ cups (600ml) milk

⅓ cup (80ml) heavy whipping cream

2 tablespoons (20g) dextrose

2 tablespoons (20g) powdered milk

¼ cup + 2 tablespoons (90g) sugar

1 vanilla bean, seeds scraped out

4½ ounces (130g) dark chocolate (at least 72% cocoa solids), broken into small pieces

INSTRUCTIONS

1. Pour the milk, cream, dextrose, powdered milk, and sugar into a small, heavy saucepan. Stir to mix all the ingredients. Bring the mixture to 180°F (85°C) (check the temperature with a probe), and then turn off the heat. Transfer the mixture to a bowl. Stir in the vanilla bean seeds and mix them in. Cover the bowl and put it in the refrigerator to cool for about 1 hour. Alternatively, pour the mixture into an ice cream maker, and freeze according to the manufacturer's instructions.

2. Once the gelato is chilled, remove the bowl from the fridge and whisk the gelato to remove any lumps. Re-cover the bowl and put it in the freezer for 3–5 hours. Whisk the gelato again every 30 minutes to remove any lumps and ensure a creamy consistency.

3. Once the gelato is ready, melt the chocolate in a small saucepan and drizzle most of it over the frozen gelato, reserving some in the pan to use as topping. Use a spatula to mix in the melted chocolate. Drizzle the last of the chocolate on top of the gelato and enjoy.

Frutti di Bosco Sorbetto

WHEN I WAS GROWING UP, WE USED TO PICK WILD BERRIES THAT GREW ALONG A TRAIL IN THE MOUNTAINS NEARBY. WHEN WE GOT HOME, WE ALWAYS MADE THIS FRESH SORBET. IT TASTES LIKE SUMMERTIME.

PREP TIME: *20 minutes* | FREEZING TIME: *3–5 hours* | SERVES: *4–6*

¾ cup (175g) sugar

1⅓ cups (315ml) water

4 cups (500g) mixed berries
 (blueberries, blackberries,
 and raspberries)

2 egg whites

INSTRUCTIONS

1. Pour the sugar and water into a heavy saucepan. Bring the mixture to a boil, constantly stirring it until the sugar has completely dissolved. Purée the berries in a blender. Pour the mixture through a coarse sieve into a bowl. Strain the purée again through a finer sieve, if you're using blueberries, to filter out the tiny seeds. Pour the berry purée into the saucepan and boil for at least 2 minutes, and then take the pan off the heat.

2. Let the berry purée cool down. Transfer it to a bowl, cover it, and put it in fridge to chill for about 1 hour. Transfer the purée to another bowl and mix it thoroughly. In a separate bowl, beat the egg whites until they are foamy. Combine the egg whites with the berry mixture and mix it well. Cover and put the bowl in the freezer for about 3–5 hours, mixing it every 30 minutes or so, to remove any lumps and ensure a smooth consistency.

Zuppa Inglese

(LIQUEUR-INFUSED SPONGE CAKE WITH CREAMY GELATO)

THIS IS A VARIATION OF MY GRANDMOTHER ROSITA'S CAKE, COMBINED WITH A CLASSIC ITALIAN GELATO. *ZUPPA INGLESE* IS LITERALLY TRANSLATED AS "ENGLISH SOUP," A DECADENT SPIN ON THE BELOVED ENGLISH TRIFLE. LEGEND HAS IT THAT THE DESSERT WAS DEVELOPED IN THE LATE SIXTEENTH CENTURY FOR ENGLISH VISITORS, WHO FREQUENTLY CAME TO ITALY TO ENJOY THE WARM CLIMATE, BUT WERE NOSTALGIC FOR A TASTE OF HOME.

PREP TIME: *50 minutes* | COOKING AND FREEZING TIME: *5–7 hours* | SERVES: *4–6*

FOR THE CREAMY GELATO

2½ cups (600ml) milk

⅓ cup (80ml) heavy whipping cream

¼ cup + 2 tablespoons (80g) sugar

2 tablespoons (20g) dextrose

2 tablespoons (20g) powdered milk

5 egg yolks

1 vanilla bean, seeds scraped out

FOR THE SPONGE CAKE

Pan di Spagna (page 150)

FOR THE ALKERMES LIQUEUR

7 tablespoons (100ml) water

5 tablespoons (60g) sugar

⅓ cup (80ml) Alkermes liqueur

FOR THE CHOCOLATE SAUCE

4½ ounces (70g) dark chocolate (at least 72% cocoa solids), broken into small pieces, melted in a heavy saucepan

INSTRUCTIONS

1. To make the gelato: Pour the milk and heavy whipping cream into a small, heavy saucepan and add the sugar, dextrose, and powdered milk. Mix in the egg yolks. Beat the mixture with a whisk, until it is thick and smooth.

2. Add the vanilla bean seeds to the pan, stirring constantly, and bring the mixture to 180°F (85°C) (not a degree more, or the eggs will coagulate; you can use a probe to take the temperature).

3. Fill a large metal bowl halfway up with ice water.

4. Turn off the heat, remove the pan from the stove, and place it in the metal bowl filled halfway with ice water. This will lower the temperature of the mixture. Keep stirring, for a few minutes, while the mixture cools. When it is cool, put it in the refrigerator to rest for at least 2 hours. Once the gelato is chilled, whisk it to remove any lumps, cover it, and put it in the freezer. Whisk the gelato every 30 minutes over the next 3–5 hours. This will help make a creamy gelato. While the gelato is freezing, start making the sponge cake.

5. To make the sponge cake: Preheat the oven to 350°F (180°C). *Prepare Pan de Spagna* (page 150).

6. Remove the sponge cake from the oven and let it cool on a rack. While the cake is cooling, prepare the Alkermes liqueur and melt the chocolate.

7. To make the Alkermes liqueur: Bring the water and sugar to a boil in a small heavy saucepan. Remove it from the heat and set it aside to cool. When the mixture is cool, stir in the Alkermes liqueur and set it aside.

8. Assembly: Cut the sponge cake into pieces and put them in a large dish. Pour the Alkermes solution on top to soak the cake.

9. Choose a pretty glass dish (some people like to use a large, tall jar to layer the ingredients) and start assembling the Zuppa Inglese: Start with a layer of creamy gelato. Next place a layer of the soaked sponge cake over the gelato and drizzle some of the melted chocolate over the sponge cake. Repeat this process until all the ingredients have been used, topping it off with the last of the melted chocolate. Freeze again before serving.

ACKNOWLEDGMENTS

Thank you to my family, friends, customers, and everyone who has supported me. Thank you to Lido Vannucchi for the beautiful photos, and to Marilyn Kretzer, Theresa Thompson, and Jennifer Williams for making this book a reality. *Grazie Mille!*

Damiano and his Grandma Rosita

Left to right: Damiano's father, Ivan; brother Massimiliano; grandma Rosita; Damiano; and Damiano's mother, Laura.

INDEX

D